George, Elise and a mandarin

Terry Fewtrell

George, Elise and a mandarin

Identity in Early Australia

Dedication

To the bearers of the story

Samuel Markus Fewtrell (1891–1988)
wonderful man and grandfather, a link to the past

and

Logan, Emily, Samuel, Daniel and Benjamin
delightful young Australians and grandchildren, beacons to the future

George, Elise and a mandarin: Identity in Early Australia
ISBN 978 1 76041 377 4
Copyright © Terry Fewtrell 2017

First published 2017 by
GINNINDERRA PRESS
PO Box 3461 Port Adelaide 5015
www.ginninderrapress.com.au

Contents

Preface		7
Introduction		9
1	'I am of Shropshire, my shins be sharp'	11
2	A smooth passage	18
3	The yeoman finds his bearings	25
4	A woman from Schleswig-Holstein	33
5	A very difficult passage	42
6	So who are George and Elise?	51
7	Quarantine and other trials	55
8	Starting to 'butty' in Homestead 4171	61
9	'This land is mine: this land is me'	67
10	A community emerges	77
11	The yeoman builds a nation	84
12	A man with wide horizons	93
13	Growing and going in all directions	100
14	A declaration and a death	107
15	Son of the father, son of the mother	114
16	Endings without meetings	123
17	Empire's reward	127
18	Identity then and now	134
Notes		142
Bibliography		156
Thanks and acknowledgements		160

Preface

Every family has stories. The characteristics and achievements of earlier generations are often handed down in fractured form – part fact, part legend, sometimes imagined interpretation. Some stories are compelling in their heroism or stoicism. Others are remarkable for their seeming ordinariness. Sometimes a photo or image is significant for what it tells or what it doesn't tell. A face, a remnant, an artefact can become a conduit to the past. Such items are cherished and often mused upon. They can become touchstones to other times and places.

This book is about all of the above and more. It is inspired by the stories of two Australian immigrants of the 1870s, George Fewtrell and Elise Bresler (Rehder), who came from different lands and backgrounds, to be challenged by adversity and ultimately to share an unlikely life together and make their contributions to Australian life.

But this story is more than a retelling of handed-down facts. It is a journey to discover more about Elise and George by better understanding the context of their lives, in both their northern and southern hemisphere settings. In this way, a far more textured picture of each emerges, which adds form and colour to the mosaic of fragments. It also facilitates a meaningful appreciation of their individual characters, the impact of place, the challenges they faced and their responses.

At its essence, therefore, this story is a study of identity and how it is affected by place, time and the emigrant experience. George Fewtrell and Elise Bresler emerge as exemplars of two different types of Australians, two different phases of Australian history. George was unquestionably British. A man with a clear identity – a son of the Empire, who invested in it and was repaid by it. By contrast, Elise was a woman from a land conflicted and long fought over, coveted by the super powers of the day. For her, identity was fragile, uncertain and potentially fleeting. She became a British Australian but held to her Schleswig-Holstein heritage. In both cases, their identities were challenged and shaped, albeit in different ways, by the lives they came to share in the great south land.

The story that emerges is in part a personal reflection on some of the formative forces that influenced two great-grandparents and perhaps, in some small part, the writer himself. There are of course other influences, other family stories, some relating to Irish convicts and Cornish miners. All are important, but the George and Elise story has always had a compelling narrative and a long-held fascination.

Identity is a curious thing. In the tribe of humanity, an individual is authentic when they become the unique person that they truly are. But who we are, essentially, is the result of the intersection of the randomness of our genetic composition and the circumstances and context in which we live our lives. It is within this conundrum that much of the complexity of the human story unfolds.

The contributions of George and Elise chronicled in this story cover the period from the 1870s to the end of the World War I. More than a century later, those contributions are still relevant in assisting Australians to gain a more nuanced understanding of the unfolding nature of Australian identity. As in the time of George and Elise, identity is an ever evolving concept.

Introduction

The day is new. The light is clear. The air is fresh, tingling with mixed aromas. In an early-morning Lahore fruit market, loose-robed vendors carry baskets of fruits on their heads as they rush to prepare their stalls for the morning's trade. Activity is everywhere but its seeming chaos is organised and businesslike.

Gradually, as the displays are settled, their activity shifts from preparation to proposition. In a repetitive almost rhythmical way, they tell the world, or at least anyone who may be passing, of their offerings, their merits and their willingness to exchange. Among the fruits they sell are mandarins, or sangtra as they are known in that part of the world.

Commercial citrus is thought to have originated in south-east Asia, among what are now the modern-day states of India, Pakistan and China. So it is no surprise that oranges and mandarins figure prominently in this, one of Pakistan's largest fruit markets. Similar scenes can be witnessed across the subcontinent. Pakistan ranks tenth on the list of mandarin producers. Annual crop production exceeds half a million metric tonnes, with an estimated 170,000 hectares under cultivation, the bulk of it in the Punjab. India, which shares the Punjab valley, boasts similar figures.

The varieties of mandarins grown today in the subcontinent are dominated by two introduced varieties: Kinnow (the most common, and sourced originally from the US) and Fewtrell's Early (from Australia). The Kinnow was developed in California in 1915 and reaches maturity in mid-season. The Fewtrell's Early was developed in Palmwoods, Queensland, around the turn of the 20th century. As the name suggests, it matures early, coming on to the market ahead of other varieties. Both were imported to the region in the 1940s, as the British-administered Punjab was looking to develop the commercial prospects of the citrus, and specifically the mandarin, industry.

That a mandarin variety, named Fewtrell, crossed from the former British colony of Queensland to enhance the development of another British dominion is a story that says much about the reach and influence of the British Empire. It is all the more a British Empire story when one considers that the man for whom the mandarin was named, George Fewtrell, came originally from England's Shropshire, at the agricultural heart of the Empire itself.

Fewtrell's Early mandarin is in many ways a symbol of the ability of the then British Empire to change the world. It did so in a way that developed know-how and skill, shared that knowledge around the globe, and in the process improved the lives of many. It also created a legacy of cooperation and understanding that persists to this day.

For George Fewtrell, such an outcome would have been improbable, even unthinkable. And yet he was a man who put his faith in the British Empire, which in turn rewarded him amply. While he did not live to see his mandarin grown in vast quantities in one of the largest citrus-growing regions of the world, he would have been content with his modest contribution to the Empire and its southern dominion. Building the British Empire was part of his unstated purpose in life.

The woman he was ultimately to marry had come from a different culture, a contested land in northern Europe. She was someone who paid dearly for her quest to the great south land. Together their stories reveal much about the early exploration of the frontiers of Australian identity.

1

'I am of Shropshire, my shins be sharp'

Shropshire's geography has shaped its history. Rolling hills and their resulting valleys and rivers tell a story of England's most land-bound county that extends deep into time. Excavations and research have peeled back the various stages of settlement and development, dating from pre-Roman times. The area has been home to various peoples, including the Saxons in the eighth century, the invading Danes in the ninth and 10th centuries and the Norman Conquest of 1066.

Through all these times, the county's rolling countryside provided hilltop fortifications for successive waves of conquerors. Those same hills, to this day, provide much of the mythology and folklore of the area. Primary amongst its topography is the Wrekin, close to the border with Wales. It is said in the county that 'a Shropshire mon is nivver lost if he con see the Wrekin'. In reality it is not an overly high point (407 metres) but has inspired much legend and myth, some involving man-eating giants. It also came to invoke much of the spiritual and cultural inspiration of the area, along with expressing symbolically the warmth of its people.

Much of the early political history of Shropshire relates to the repulsion of incursions from Welsh tribes, manifested in both physical barriers (dykes and ditches) and legal constraints. But trade and movement between the peoples of Wales and of Shropshire has been a constant throughout the centuries. One prominent identity well known on both sides of the border, in both life and death, was St Winefred, a seventh-century Welsh Christian woman. Reputedly the daughter of a Welsh nobleman, she became an abbess. Nearly 400 years after her death, her remains were for a time relocated to Shrewsbury, the Shropshire capital. Various wells and shrines emerged at places along the route in Shropshire, with which her name and memory have continued associations.

Not only do rivers, most notably the Severn, accompany the hills, but the landscape was blessed with good soils and an abundance and diversity of minerals. Over time, this meant that the agricultural produce of its soils found ready markets beyond neighbouring counties. Significantly it also created the circumstances where the valleys of Shropshire would become the birthplace of the industrial revolution. From the early 1800s, life began to change significantly as the Severn became the life stream of not just agricultural but also industrial production. Focused in Ironbridge Gorge, the river provided the setting for the fusion of iron, coal and tar and the transportation of the products that emerged from those processes.

This was change that would advance the Empire and drive it to become the world's first industrial superpower. What was happening in Shropshire's valleys would take the British Empire to its greatest heights. To be a Shropshire lad at this time was to be a man of the Empire – a deliverer of change and progress. Shropshire was British and the British were shaping and changing the world. One's identity could not have been clearer.

But other changes were also on the way, thanks to a fabled son of Shropshire, Charles Darwin. Born in February 1809 to a wealthy Shrewsbury family, with a rich intellectual pedigree, the young Charles took most of his schooling in the city of his birth. His family had property and farms in the district and he had plenty of opportunity to observe the cycle of agricultural work involved in maintaining the family estates. Darwin was an acute observer of nature, spending years of research and observation before he committed his thoughts to paper in what became his seminal work, *On the Origin of Species*, published in 1859. By that time, he had spent years at university in Edinburgh and Cambridge, travelled the world on HMS *Beagle* and documented endless observations of the patterns and behaviours of the natural world. The outcome and findings of his work rocked the scientific world, causing shock waves that would run currents into virtually all aspects of life and mankind's understanding of the world and itself.

Significantly, when Darwin came to write his book, he deliberately began with the simplest of examples, based on his observations of farm workers that had begun in his youth in Shropshire. His plan was to introduce the reader gradually to his concept of species development by starting with examples that virtually all would recognise, as not just believable, but familiar. To do so, he instanced common practices of choosing certain animals and plants that had desirable characteristics and breeding from them, in the hope and expectation based on past experience that such traits would be strengthened and become dominant. The first chapter of the work is entitled 'Variation under Domestication'. In this he used examples of plant and animal breeding that produced variations, reinforced over several breeding cycles to achieve significant, if not dramatic, change.

In this way, Darwin was able to tap into the known lived experience of the common man to lay out a principle on which he progressively built his thesis of natural selection. Selection was something that the agricultural worker understood and practised. It was not too large a leap to then move to selection that was determined by other natural factors. Darwin used the humble strawberry as an example, writing,

> As soon, however, as gardeners picked out individual plants with slightly larger, earlier, or better fruit, and raised seedlings from them, and again picked out the best seedlings and bred from them, then there appears (aided by some crossing with distinct species) those many admirable varieties of strawberry which have been raised during the last thirty or forty years.

George Fewtrell would have been 15 years old when *On the Origin of Species* was published. He is unlikely to have read the book, but by then he had commenced his own life's work as an agricultural labourer.

No doubt he would have been learning the very same techniques and practices for developing improved plant species that Darwin had observed on the farms around Shropshire in his youth. George was destined to spend a lifetime plying these crafts with his hands and applying the practice-based principle that his county's more famous son had articulated.

Darwin's work was also underwritten by another truth – that species are not set in stone but, to use his word, are 'plastic'. By this he meant they were able to be shaped and fashioned into something that, although similar, was in fact quite different, perhaps ultimately in a radical sense. Here he seems to be referring to what one Darwin scholar has described as 'the principle, namely the cumulative power of selection, by which good breeders succeed'. This message would have a remarkable relevance to the life that lay ahead of George Fewtrell. Ultimately, George would succeed as a breeder to develop a variety of fruit with sufficiently different characteristics to ensure its commercial success and adoption in different environments. In so doing, it would contribute to improving the diet of millions.

Little is known of George's life in Shropshire, apart from the fact that he was one of 11 children, born to Samuel and Maria Fewtrell in 1842 or '43 at Munslow, not far west of Ironbridge Gorge. The couple were married in 1837, George being their third child and one of five boys. Samuel was himself a man of Shropshire, believed to have been born in 1815 at Shipton, about 10 kilometres south-west of the market town of Much Wenlock. It would seem that he had not travelled far by the time he married Maria Harris, as George's birthplace lies just a few more kilometres to the south. Samuel is variously described as an agricultural labourer or a farm bailiff, the latter term denoting a greater degree of skill or responsibility.

George followed in his father's footsteps, probably almost literally, as his stated occupation was agricultural labourer. He is known to have spent time in some of the more southerly parts of Shropshire, including Leintwardine, which straddles the neighbouring county of

Herefordshire. Wherever he may have been, given the nature of his work, George would have participated in the annual hiring ritual to gain employment with a farm owner. These hiring fairs were known colloquially as 'mops' and took place either at Christmas time or, in the south of the county, in May. The hiring was done on a year to year basis, starting either in early January or after the harvest was completed in mid-year.

While this sounds like an early version of a careers exhibition or job expo, it was in fact highly class-bound. From the worker's perspective, it involved a search for a considerate and tolerable master. The quality of food and lodging, along with the level of wages, were key determinants of employment preferences. A ballad of the day, called 'Country Hirings', expressed some of the anxiety of the process:

> Servant men, stand up for your wages.
> When to the hiring you do go,
> For you must work all sorts of weather,
> Both cold and wet and snow.

Often, workers would accept a lower rate of pay as a trade-off to the inclusion of a get-out clause in their contract. The whole process was a one-sided oral exchange, sealed by a handshake or a nod. There was no recording of the detail and no redress if the farmer chose later not to honour any aspect of the deal. Sometimes when the negotiation for a new yearly contract was concluded early in the hiring fair, the employer would advance the worker a shilling as a way of sealing the deal and securing the employee's unconditional commitment to honour the arrangement. Such payments were known as an earnest.

Housing was a troubled area of negotiation, with some offering inferior accommodation or cottages. The standard wage level for farm labourers in southern Shropshire in 1872 was nine shillings per week, with an extra shilling if Sunday work was required. For married men with children, there were added difficulties, due to the cost of accommodation and schooling. In most cases, much depended on the generosity of the employer, and this was often a determining factor in whether a worker signed on again for another year. This left most farm labourers in a fickle and capricious predicament. In some parts, illiterate labourers were considered the best workers, which in turn developed attitudes that the children of such employees should be encouraged to join the workforce as early as possible, with 10 years being considered an appropriate age. The implication of these attitudes was that some masters saw education as an impediment to cheap labour.

Clearly, George Fewtrell would have been aware of these difficulties as he faced his 30th birthday and assessed his circumstances and prospects. He was single but probably contemplated marriage at some stage. His future in the land where he was raised would inevitably mean working for a gentleman farmer, with all the deference that accompanied it, and for meagre rewards and little chance of becoming his own master and building his own enterprise. In any case, he would have wondered about the future of agricultural work amidst the growing industrial focus in the valleys. On the other hand, amidst this growing uncertainty and agitation for better conditions locally, there was another alternative. Migration agents, working on behalf of the government of the colony of Queensland, had begun campaigns to attract workers to that part of the Empire. It was a long way away, but that was no impediment to a healthy young single man.

What would have made it particularly attractive was that the government of Queensland was specifically seeking agricultural workers, genuine yeoman farmers, to build the fortunes of this distant land. Emigration agents for Queensland, who were promoting emigration in agricultural communities, would no doubt have been outlining pay rates available in the colony. These compared favourably with the nine shillings per week that was the going rate on Shropshire farms. Rates quoted in the *Queensland Agent-General's Handbook* for potential emigrants, as recorded on 24 May 1875, stated that the average wages of farm labourers in Queensland were £35–40 per annum (with rations) for a single man and between £45 and $50 per annum (with rations) for a married man. These rates would have been very similar to those considered by George when deciding to emigrate.

It is not known what level of schooling George Fewtrell had received. He could read and write but the extent of his numeracy, other learning skills and general knowledge, remains unclear, although his subsequent life and achievements suggests he was more than capable and competent in many areas. He seems indeed to have had sharp shins. Adventure and the discovery of new horizons seemed on his agenda. He possessed tradable work skills that perhaps one day would enable him to be his own master. If he were to have a family, he probably figured they faced better prospects in the warmth of Queensland, rather than the cold of Shropshire. And besides he would still be an Englishman, albeit one in the Antipodes. He would just be in a different part of the British Empire. He would be the yeoman farmer that the Queensland government was seeking to play a part in conquering a new land and building a new society. It was 1873 and George Fewtrell was bound for Moreton Bay.

2

A smooth passage

European emigrants in the 1870s had many choices. In general, the broader social conditions created a disposition to go. The next question was to where? The bulk of the movement of peoples at this time was east to west, with America and to some degree Canada exciting the interest and attracting the commitment of most. Apart from its great allure of freedom and success, the greatest practical advantage that the US had in the migration stakes was that it involved only a three- to four-week sailing journey, as against a four-month passage south to Australia. This situation was exacerbated by the fact that at this time most passages to the US were via steamships, while voyages south were typically on smaller, and slower, sail-powered vessels. These time variations did not just mean longer exposure to the perils of the sea, but an extended period of lost earning capacity.

Weighing against this natural competitive advantage was the matter of cost. The potential opportunity costs included the loss of relationships, the likely degree of strangeness of the destination measured against the person's fear of change and the unknown, and lastly, the actual expenditure the migrant had to outlay. This is what constituted the crude emigration equation. Potentially the greatest leverage that Australian colonies had in its calculation was the free passage offered by some. The Queensland government's offer of free passage to migrants was, in simple terms, a response to market forces. The market in human cargo and aspirations was indeed competitive. It was for this reason that immigration agents and promotional campaigns were undertaken by various colonies in the mid-1800s. Following its separation from NSW in 1859, the Queensland government's top priority was to recruit people to its vast, seemingly empty, lands.

Figures on 19th-century migration from European countries reveal that it ramped up significantly in the decade 1871–1880 and peaked in the following decade. This applied to England, Germany and Denmark. There was good reason why migration to Australia would have increased in this period. Studies have since revealed that Australia in 1870 was the richest country in the world, in fact more than 70% above the average of other nations. Not that such marketing information was available or known at the time. Nonetheless, the various Australian colonies needed to compete among themselves and against other major destinations.

Throughout the decade of the 1870s, Queensland government migration programs were active, although the offer of free passage was on and off at times during that period due to the government's recurring financial crises. When available, free passage was offered to single men, agricultural or farm labourers (with not more than two children under 12 years of age) and to single women who were domestic servants, and married women. Those granted free passage were required to pay £1, which covered bedding, other victuals, medical treatment on the voyage and temporary accommodation on arrival at the port of disembarkation.

The rhetoric of the recommendations to potential emigrants was unrestrained. One advocate had no doubt that

> the road seems so clear to success and fortune in Queensland, that it is indeed a matter of surprise that any difficulty is experienced in England in persuading people to come at once to such a prosperous and flourishing country.

This was backed up by fulsome testimonials, such as that of Andrew Gurdler in a letter of appreciation to activist emigration agent, F.W. Hetherington:

I got into work as soon as we landed in Brisbane in the depot... I only wish I had come out here before as I am getting my 7s per day for eight hours... Everything is so cheap out here; you can buy horses for 10s each. You can get a house and eight acres of land for £7 a year; you cannot rent a house in England for that money. I should like for any working man to come out here – not to work for 15s a week when they can get it in two days out here. Who would not come to Queensland, Sir? I am 18 miles north of Brisbane, what they call Pine River. Tell them all to come out here to do well and to save a fortune, and not starve in England as they do.

For George Fewtrell, navigating the bureaucratic requirements was relatively easy. He submitted his papers through the itinerant immigration agent of the Queensland government, perhaps by post to the Agent General in London, awaited advice of acceptance and then presented himself at the London docks for embarkation. As a single man on a free passage, he would travel steerage and looked forward to what was the adventure before the adventure. He was off to the Antipodes, but he knew he was going to a place that seemed not unlike England. The language, law and currency were all basically the same as he had known all his life. It was, after all, part of the Empire. There would clearly be much that was strange and new, but equally a great deal would be similar. His confidence rose as he read in the documents that he would be travelling on the cutter *Winefred*, departing from London docks on 4 October 1873. The cutter's name would no doubt have attracted his interest and a wry smile, as he recognised that Winefred was a friend of Shropshire and surely would look after this son of the county.

At age 30, George was one of the more mature unmarried males on the journey. Coming from an agricultural setting, he was unaccustomed to sea travel and onboard living, but his curiosity made him an engaged passenger, observant and helpful, exploring the vessel and following the rituals and routines of ship life and the progress of the passage. He observed closely the procedures involved in departing the docks and guiding the ship through the channel of the Thames.

Before long, the ship's surgeon was instructing each group of passengers on the sanitation and cleaning procedures required for the journey. Passengers were strongly encouraged to rise early, leave their compartments as soon as practical and remain on deck as long as possible. They were also encouraged to take with them their linen and bedding so they could be aired on the decks. Partitions in the various compartments were completely taken down in order to maximise fresh air ventilation.

While somewhat onerous, these protocols provided a degree of insurance against the ravages of disease. They were the hallmark of a well-managed ship and an effective master and surgeon relationship. They also helped to create a broader community of travellers, enabling passengers to mix more easily and make new friendships. Morale on a journey as long as this was important for all.

Despite best endeavours, disease inevitably occurred. An outbreak of scarlet fever in two families led to them being quarantined in the ship's hospital, their bedding destroyed and the compartments disinfected and whitewashed. An outbreak of typhus fever involving a passenger in the single men's compartment led to more drastic action. The affected compartment was cleaned with great vigour, a process extending over some days, with the passengers bringing their goods and chattels on deck to be in the fresh air and sunlight and forced to spend the night camping there. The patient was removed to one of the lifeboats, where a temporary hospital was set up. Despite the best efforts of the crew, the man died within a few days.

Such incidents were of particular concern in the early stages of the journey, as the ship approached the equator and entered a zone of breathless air and becalmed seas. It was at this stage of the journey that emigrant ships most resembled a floating rag-fair, with passengers' linen and bedding brought up from the oppressively humid quarters below, and hung from all manner of places on deck, in order to air in the sun and reduce the risk of disease.

George took a particular interest in the activities on the quarterdeck, the stage for many social and maritime rituals of the journey. The noon formalities, involving the captain and one or two of the mates assembling with sextants and quadrants, were one such activity. There they proceeded to take measurements and adjust instruments and after a short time one would announce to his confrères and the assembled passengers that it was noon. This somewhat solemn procedure was significant in that it marked the beginning of another day on the journey. Passage of time was then measured by a sandglass until the group assembled again on the deck with their instruments.

As the voyage progressed, George, like his fellow travellers, slowly adjusted to the reality that while their world grew larger each passing day, the elements that defined that world grew less. It was not long before, each day on looking out, they saw only the sun, the moon, the sea and the horizon. Even the familiar stars of the northern skies at night sank lower in the sky each evening.

An occasional opening onto their world was provided by the sight of another ship, homeward bound to London. Often, particularly when in the windless doldrums, contact would be made so that reports of each other's progress could be passed to authorities. Passengers were encouraged to write letters home to family, so that these could also be passed to the returning ships for forwarding through the mail.

By all accounts, George was always keen to talk with strangers and fellow travellers. Living in close quarters with others with whom he was unacquainted, he engaged freely with them, eager to hear of their plans and pick up snippets of information and advice. He was a man on the move, literally, and he was thinking of, if not planning, his future in this faraway land named for the Queen. Victoria would be sovereign there, just as she was in Shropshire. He was in his prime and primed to make a contribution. No doubt he took some interest in the passengers from the single women's compartment. Perhaps he might soon find a suitable woman, marry and have children. He knew that he possessed the skills that his new homeland needed and he looked forward to being his own man, his own master – to be the yeoman farmer on his own land. Life was full of hope and opportunity. It was exciting. Enjoy the passage and then dive into it!

It seems the *Winefred* had a relatively smooth and uneventful passage. The ship was seen as a model for the emigration trade – specifically designed with the latest of features, able to convey 500 passengers safely in a well rigged vessel with a well drilled crew. The *Winefred* made several voyages to Brisbane, becoming known as the *Winefred* Marvel – the pride of the Empire. It was immortalised by one passenger as follows:

> When swiftly sailing o'er the main,
> Old England lost to view,
> One thought shall cheer us on our way,
> One hope sustains us through.
> Although we leave our native land,
> And parting tears have shed,
> We're bound for anew and happy land'
> In the good ship *Winefred*.
> New faces soon will welcome us,
> Across the mighty main,
> And if we leave dear ones behind,
> New friends we hope to gain.
> And when our new home's shore shall loom,
> With Brisbane's port ahead,
> We will give a last and parting cheer,
> For the good ship *Winefred*.

George arrived at Moreton Bay on 14 January 1874. After the formalities and retrieval of his goods, he made his way to the government depot that provided board and lodging for migrants on arrival in Brisbane. Here he launched into the throng of new arrivals and those old hands who knew the ropes. This was above all an information exchange, a place to stay for around 10 days while he got his bearings, learned from those who had arrived before him and plan his next move. These lodgings, food included, enabled him to seek out some opportunities for employment, or work out where he might usefully focus his efforts.

It was now up to him to make contacts, soak up information and exercise the best judgements he could as to how to make his way in this new country. He may have had occasion to pause and recall at times the reassuring advice in the Agent General's handbook for emigrants:

> Labour is wanted, employment is offered, wages are good and food is cheap. A working man, with sober habits, can rise to independence and comfort. Above all, he is relieved from the anxiety about the future of his children, who are away from the overcrowded market of Europe.

3

The yeoman finds his bearings

The first few days of an emigrant's life in their new homeland are ones of sensory, intellectual and emotional overload. So much to take in, to sort and make sense of, and begin to build a framework of how things work, what is important and immediately useful – in order to form a reliable basis on which to make judgements and decisions. In his mind, George had prepared for this time. He was a practical man, methodical and calm, not impulsive or given to emotional display. He would deal with the realities that he faced.

The most immediate of those realities was the climate. Arriving in the middle of a Brisbane January was an inevitable shock to the constitution. Dealing with the heat of the day was one thing, but the humidity of the night was perhaps worse. He had heard and read of the climatic conditions, but now he was experiencing the real difference between Shropshire and Queensland. Given his occupation, he may have had some foreboding about working on open farmland in such conditions. A greater consideration, however, would have been where and how he would find such work.

The campaign to recruit agricultural workers as migrants was part of a broad strategy to diversify the state's economy and break the stranglehold that pastoralists had over the economy and the electoral system. That strength was built on the waves of pastoral expansion that fanned out from the New South Wales border, proceeding ever north and westwards. Cattle and ultimately sheep stations would dominate the landscape, driving a frontier that marked the line of colonial claims and indigenous eviction. The Darling Downs to the west of Brisbane became the power centre for pastoralist interests, an entrenched elite since the time of official separation from New South Wales. Increasingly, the city folk of Brisbane and Ipswich, with their commercial and professional focus, resented this sway and the landed gentry swagger that accompanied it.

The call for yeomanry, to which George had enlisted, was at the centre of political debate and manoeuvring that preoccupied Brisbane and colonial affairs for much of the period between 1860 and the 1890s. It was a cause that drew supporters from across both the political boundaries and colonial borders. Among the protagonists for a yeoman farmer future were noted republicans John Dunmore Lang and Daniel Deniehy.

Lang, who was active in the Queensland debates, had a particular loathing for the big pastoralists. Deniehy, while NSW-based, looked beyond the then colonial governance framework to envisage what one observer has described as 'an Australian community of independent yeoman farmers'. While his vision was irresistibly utopian, Deniehy saw the role of the yeoman farmer as a key ingredient of a successful economic and social order. He defined the yeoman farmer's contribution to that republican order as follows:

> ...we consider the Small Settler a very important personage. He comes to this colony possessed of the ability and industry so earnestly desired, and all the requirements so much needed, or in plainer terms, he has the knack of converting a wilderness into a profitable and comfortable homestead, advantageous to himself and those around him; he brings his produce into the nearest township to where he locates; he gets a ready purchase for his commodities, and he then returns to his labour, after purchasing whatever articles he may require from the storekeeper or others in the township.

In this vision, the yeoman farmer is the bedrock element of society and the economy at the local and broader levels. A necessary first step in achieving this was the unlocking of the land, which in the Queensland context meant overcoming the power of the pastoralists.

In Queensland, these arguments played out against a boom and bust economic and financial environment that afflicted the fledgling colony. George Fewtrell was fortunate that he arrived in Brisbane during an economic boom, although one that turned sour shortly afterwards in 1876. An enthusiasm for progress led successive governments into overly ambitious projects, such as railway developments, and crippling debt which then stumbled into depression. These factors were indicative of the type of background regarding his new home that George was unlikely to have known or appreciated before leaving England.

In fact, there was much of which George most likely was unaware regarding his chosen destination. It would have been clear that the Queensland government was engaged in the largest recruitment of emigrants in the Australian colonial period – the state population increasing from 30,000 in 1861 to 394,000 in 1891. The lesser known reality, however, was that at the same time the Queensland authorities were complicit in and ultimately responsible for the forced removal and large-scale deaths of the Aboriginal people who had previously held custody of the lands that became, in colonial terms, Queensland. Such was the prevailing mindset of 19th century colonial society that a 'run them out and bring them in' approach was something that just had to happen. The Native Police, originally established by the NSW government before separation, played a significant and ruthless role in this process, becoming effectively the first element of land policy under the Queensland government.

The battle to attract and establish a cohort of independent yeoman farmers was as much about transplanting British values, as it was about diversifying the state's economic base. It was also driven by a view that smallholding settlements, engaged in the cultivation of crops, represented the authentic form of colonisation. Such endeavours would involve independent landowners engaged in an honourable working of the earth to sustain the community. It was also expressive of a view that criticised many pastoralists for having a simple and single-minded exploitative view of the land. In advancing these objectives, much of the vision was also an opportunity to replicate the broad proportions of English, Welsh, Scottish and Irish in the Queensland corner of the Empire.

However, this latter aim was usurped by the overwhelming need to attract settlers, so long as they were Caucasian. The need to counter rising populations of Chinese and Melanesian arrivals, along with Aboriginal numbers, was the basis for this imperative. Northern Europeans were seen as potentially suitable emigrants and between 1860 and 1880, 17,000 German and other European settlers arrived. So effective were the initiatives that by 1881 Queensland had become home to the largest number of German-born residents of all the Australian colonies. Ultimately by the early 1880s, Queensland would have the most multicultural society of all the Australian colonies.

The vision of the yeoman farmer was part of the competing futures for the colony, advanced by the key political protagonists of the time, led by conservative and pastoralist-aligned Thomas McIlwraith and the Brisbane-based Liberal Samuel Griffith. Despite their differences, both were driven by the shared imperative for progress. Successive land reform initiatives broke much of the power of the pastoralists, opening land under lease or licence to smaller selectors for agricultural purposes. Not that the life of the small landholder farmer was an easy one. Various clusters of development started and then struggled or ended in failure. Climatic and soil conditions proved challenging and often confounding, depending on the crop and the location. As Anthony Trollope observed following his visit to Australia in the early 1870s, 'Land is cheap because the struggle required to make it useful is severe.'

Little is known of where and how George Fewtrell spent his first year or two in the colony. He is known to have worked for some time in the Toowoomba region, perhaps on the railway extension or in early farmer settlements among the nearby agricultural areas, and at Mt Cotton south of Brisbane and other places on the outskirts of Brisbane.

It seems that George really was a man who knew his mind and acted decisively on his judgements. It also seems that marriage really was on George's emigration agenda. He had met Maria Taylor of Bundamba, west of Brisbane, who became the object of his affections and his wife on 24 April 1875. The couple were married in South Brisbane and they set up home on the edge of the city, with George gaining employment in nearby farming areas. A daughter, Elizabeth, was born on 2 January 1876. Sadly, the infant died three months later. A second daughter, named after her mother, was born in October 1877, followed by a son, Henry, in May of 1879.

At an early stage of his Queensland life, George was already engaged in civic affairs. He had joined the Protestant Alliance Friendly Society of Australasia (PAFSOA), which during the 1870s was in the process of establishing a network of lodges across Brisbane and Ipswich. The PAFSOA had begun in Victoria in the 1860s as an association of Protestant interests opposed to attempts by Catholics 'to get introduced into our National School curriculum the dogmas of the Roman Church'. The society achieved this objective but, preferring to be ever vigilant for their cause, was reluctant to disband. Ultimately they decided to form themselves into a friendly society and put the energies and funds of their members into supporting similarly minded members of the community, who might have need for some assistance.

The friendly societies were the welfare system of the times. They established sick funds and relief funds that supported the families of members and others in the community who suffered privations, especially during difficult economic times. Their work was essentially humanitarian and compassionate, within the sectarian framework of the times. They were broad community organisations that had youth arms and were open to female members. The society was also active in establishing patriotic funds. At its heart PAFSOA was '…essentially loyal and patriotic and our vow of loyalty to the Protestant Crown of England was honoured by our members…' George was an obviously committed member and active in the formation of one of the lodges, the Ark of Safety Lodge in South Brisbane.

It was a census year in Queensland in 1881 and no doubt George and Maria were looking forward to adding another child to the state's tally and the Empire's glory. However, little could George have imagined that by the time the numbers were tallied he would have a third daughter for only three days in September and by the end of that month his wife would be dead. Both mother and baby were victims of the curse of childbirth gone wrong.

At this point, George's world shattered. Along with his wife and daughter, all of his hopes and plans seemed also to have died. He now had to care for his young family of two children under four years of age, but he would also have to continue working to do so. A daunting task in such an era, especially for a man who came alone to the colony, with no extended family who could assist with care and child-raising tasks.

Among the friends and acquaintances George had met during his now eight years in the colony, one man stands out as a person with whom he forged a lifelong association and whose influence and support significantly altered his prospects. Peter Kuskopf had emigrated in 1865 from Schleswig-Holstein, a disputed part of the world, torn between the claims and influences of Denmark and Germany. Kuskopf was a man of many interests, lots of connections, unbounded energy and optimism. He was eight years older than George and despite their different nationalities, the two obviously shared much in terms of their outlook, openness to other people and new ideas and a desire to succeed, combined with a determination to contribute to building their pioneer communities.

Peter Kuskopf was not one to let the grass grow under his feet. He arrived in Brisbane with his wife and young family in 1865. His wife's family had decided to migrate en masse, with two males having travelled in advance of the main party to secure appropriate accommodation and arrangements. Peter Kuskopf therefore arrived in Brisbane with a network of contacts and ample local information. He established himself within the German speaking community as a man with drive and ideas, someone who could make things happen and

Peter and Catherina Kuskopf, with the six sons from Peter's first marriage and the four daughters born to Catherina. (From The Palmwoods Story.)

give wise advice. In the course of the next 40 years, he would make good use of these talents in a range of occupations, investments and particularly his offspring, who numbered 11.

In his early years in the colony, Kuskopf worked as an agricultural labourer, spending time in the Toowoomba area, Mt Cotton and Logan River, areas in which the German community figured prominently. It is likely that the friendship between George Fewtrell and Peter Kuskopf began in such a setting. Peter would seem just the sort of person George would have sought out on arrival in Brisbane. Someone who shared his ethos, was well connected, knew how to get progress on issues and keen to build a community of family and friends. Although identified as German-born, Peter Kuskopf was already a British subject by the time he met George, having been naturalised in September 1876. They were both committed to the Empire, George by birth, Peter by choice.

Now faced with personal tragedy, George would have remembered that in 1879 Peter Kuskopf's wife, Telsche, had died in childbirth, leaving him with seven children. He also would have noted, perhaps as characteristic of Peter, that within two months he had married again, to another member of the German, in fact Schleswig-Holstein, community – Catherina Rehder. Catherina was from Kellinghusen, a town in central Holstein that was only 50 kilometres from his own birthplace in Hemme.

Indeed, it is very likely that by this time George had met Catherina several times in the course of his associations with Peter Kuskopf. Peter no doubt would have offered George great sympathy and perhaps advice, as someone who had prevailed in a similar predicament. In fact, by 1881 it seems that Peter had two ideas that he thought might interest George. One was the prospect of acquiring land inland from the coast about 100 kilometres north of Brisbane. The second was that his new wife had a sister who was a widow, now living alone. Her story was poignant, she had endured much, but perhaps she might be interested in helping George as a housekeeper. It might be good for both of them.

4

A woman from Schleswig-Holstein

In February 1881, Catherina Kuskopf gave birth to a daughter, Anna. Her joy at this event would have been tinged by the knowledge that her own circumstances were now radically different to, indeed the complete opposite of, those of her younger sister, Elise. Catherina had a particular sense of responsibility for Elise, whom she had accompanied to Queensland in what became an ill-fated quest for life in the new world. Catherina had no doubt formed her own assessment of George's character. Maybe she and Peter both saw and wondered about the possibility? Perhaps Catherina was the person to first broach the idea with Peter and then with Elise?

We do not know the circumstances in which George and Elise met. However, it seems most likely that Peter and Catherina Kuskopf were instrumental, either directly or incidentally. For George, the immediate need was for support in the house and with the children. Elise's greatest need was some form of security, a place where she could fulfil a useful role in safety and work out what might be best for her in all her circumstances.

Those circumstances were that she was a widow who carried the legacy of a broken hip from an accident on a harrowing journey south. Life had left her heartbroken and depressed. She had had three children but none survived. The love of life had drained from her. The outlook for her in this still unfamiliar place was not good, perhaps bleak. Her life had taken such a dramatically different path to the one upon which she had embarked with much hope and optimism. She had been alone now for just on a year. Trying to find her way through the fog of grief and abandonment was difficult enough. She needed a fresh start, a distraction at least, and a chance to build some reserves and resilience.

In recent times, she had taken to thinking fondly of her earlier life with Catherina in Kellinghusen, in the heart of Holstein – a town on the river Stor, about 40 kilometres north-west of Hamburg, with a 750-year history. Kellinghusen sits on land that rises gently to the north, but the town is oriented to the south. Facing south meant that is was linked physically and perhaps symbolically, with the busy and ever widening course of the river Elbe, as it opens to the North Sea and the wider world beyond.

In earlier times, the Elbe spread extensively across the lowlands and Kellinghusen had its own port. Its position as a port facility, next to crossroads, meant it served as a transport link for the surrounding area. Up until 1862, ships with a draught of 1.05 metres could navigate the Kellinghusen port. Nowadays there is no evidence of such infrastructure. But Kellinghusen in the 1800s, although a minor settlement, was open to the world. It had long been a garrison town, a product in part of its strategic location at the intersection of water and land transport routes. Its inhabitants were all too familiar with demands and pressures of the larger powers that adjoined their world. Hamburg, a relatively short distance away, was a Hanseatic port accustomed to trading in the goods and ideas of the world and a city with which the Rehder family had links.

Kellinghusen was a small town in the much fought-over peninsula straddling Denmark and the German Confederation. The twin provinces of Schleswig-Holstein considered themselves inseparable, but in that strong association lay the reason for the turmoil that would afflict their people and the governance of the area for most of the 19th century. Each province felt anchored to the mass of its adjacent national power – Schleswig to Denmark and Holstein to Germany/Prussia, and yet neither wanted to be separated from the other. Eventually, Denmark and Prussia fought over the provinces from 1848 to 1850, with Prussia emerging victorious but forced to sign an agreement (the London Protocol of 1852) that effectively returned the provinces to Denmark, which in turn agreed not to tie Schleswig more closely to Denmark than to its sister duchy of Holstein.

In 1863, Denmark effectively reneged on this agreement and again the protagonists were at war, briefly, in 1864. This time the agreed outcome was that Denmark would cede both provinces to Austria and Prussia. Soon after that agreement, Prussia despatched the Austrians in a short (seven-week) war and took control of both provinces. Hovering behind the scenes throughout had been the British, concerned that the loss of the provinces to the German Confederation would significantly enhance its naval power and reach. The circumstances and history of the conflict had consumed much British diplomatic effort and eventually played into the strategic manoeuvrings leading to World War I. The issue was extremely vexed and ultimately its final resolution would involve plebiscites in both provinces in 1920, and the adjustment of national borders to reflect the majority preferences of those in the extremities of each province.

The flat terrain of Schleswig-Holstein differed greatly from the rolling hills and relative peace of the English countryside in the latter part of the 19th century. Identity in Schleswig-Holstein was not fixed but fiercely contested. It was based on an association with place and region. The framework of a nation state was fragile and always up for dispute or negotiation. It could change, depending on the strength of the latest military force to come through. Here identity was less certain, more ambiguous, perhaps conflicted and compromised. Sometimes it was better not mentioned.

In the mid-1860s, Kellinghusen had a population of 2,153. The town census of 1860 records that house number 17 was occupied by the Rehder family, but it also housed a large number of others, having 19 occupants in total. The owner was Markus (Marx) Rehder, a cabinetmaker, and Anna, his wife, who had four daughters. The daughters were Catherina, Engel (or Angela) Elise (known as Elise),

Bertha and Maria, aged respectively 15, 12, eight and three. Elise had been born, presumably in that house, on 10 September 1847. Others recorded as being at the house included two apprentice boys, a maidservant, a shoemaker's assistant, a locksmith, a blacksmith's assistant, four boarders and a married couple. Whether all of these actually lived at the house is unclear. By the time of the next census in 1864, 10 occupants were recorded, who included only the two youngest daughters, Bertha and Maria. Certainly by 1864 Catherina would have been 21 and Elise 19. No record is evident in either census of the only known boy in the family, Gustav, who in age appears to have been between Elise and Bertha.

The house, located in the lower end of the town, served as both residence and workplace for Markus's cabinet making business. Markus bought the property in 1843 from another cabinetmaker who used the premises in a similar way. Markus, while not born in Kellinghusen, had lived in the town since he was 18, when he was apprenticed to a man named Hans Lahann, described as a cooper/tubber. His wife was Magdalena Rehder, suggesting some familial link. The Lahann residence was in Lindenstrasse, a main thoroughfare which rises gently to the north of the town centre. In fact, the house that Markus Rehder bought for his family and business is located in Hauptstrasse (today No. 52), which links directly, via a sweeping curve at the foot of the church, to Lindenstrasse. Now in midlife, Markus seemingly knew Kellinghusen well and owned two other properties in the town.

The Rehder family home was a vibrant place in the 1850s to 1870s. One can imagine the bustle and activity of the family and added to that there would have been many comings and goings in a household of nearly 20, most of whom it appears were young and unmarried. For the two older girls, there would have been ample opportunity for social engagement, at least within the broader household, although neither was quick to marry and start an independent life. Catherina had left the family home to work in Hamburg for a wealthy family. It is interesting, perhaps significant, that Elise, the younger of the two, was the first to marry. She married a young man named Carl Friederich Bresler in Kellinghusen on 21 November 1875, when she was 28. He was 23. Their first child, a boy whom they named Paul, was born the following August.

Little is known of Carl Bresler. He was a tailor by occupation. Records indicate that he was born in Silesia in 1852. These two facts provide scope for some inevitable speculation. His date of birth indicates that he was at least four years younger than Elise. It is possible that he may have captured the heart of his older bride. Maybe he was a charmer or a dasher, full of life and energy. Perhaps she had watched her older sister reach her 30th year unmarried and, determined to not let that happen to her, decided on the young man from Silesia. It seems more likely, however, that the union was more a love match than anything else. It is quite possible that Carl excited Elise in lots of ways, with a bravado and confidence that belied his years, boosted her confidence and won her affections.

The fact that Carl was born in Silesia, a region locked between the modern-day states of Germany, the Czech Republic and Poland, is even more intriguing. At the time it was a province of the German Confederation. By being in Schleswig-Holstein, he was far from home, but obviously his future wife was attraction enough for him to stay. Quite possibly he had met Elise while undertaking military service in Kellinghusen and the attractions of Elise led him to stay on in the town.

It would seem that he had a somewhat adventurous spirit, such that would lead him to venture to the other side of the world with his young family. Both he and Elise did not seem hesitant to chance their arm in the world. Given the times, Carl most likely was the instigator of the emigration plan. Perhaps he was wanting to escape. If he reluctantly undertook his military service, he may have been somewhat disillusioned with life, not just in Schleswig-Holstein but Prussia as a whole, on completion of that service. He may have thought that they would struggle to raise a family there on his wage as a tailor. It may have been attractive to strike out in another place, far away and free from the ever familiar cycle of war.

The Rehder family in Kellinghusen, c. early 1870s. (Photo: Detlev Vahlendick)

The Rehder family: reading meaning into fragments

One of the very few family fragments from Elise's life is a photograph of what appears to be the family, seemingly taken as a memento of some significant occasion. No individuals are identified, but we can deduce some things from observation and intuit others from fragments of information.

Markus and Anna sit centre – they are the progenitors of this family group. Two young women sit to their immediate right and left. Clearly they are the principal focus of the picture. Each is dressed in a long skirt and white blouse. The one on the right of the picture could be said to be slightly older. The one on the left is linked, by a hand on the back of her chair, to the young man who stands beside her. He wears a uniform that has been confirmed as typical of military attire at the time. But his pose is hardly military; rather, his crossed feet and right hand tucked into his coat suggest a degree of attitude, maybe defiance. Perhaps he was some form of military reservist, required reluctantly to undertake certain army training and to wear the uniform but not committed to it. Perhaps he preferred, literally, to be somewhere else. The others in the photograph would appear to be younger siblings, including brother Gustav.

As records indicate that Anna died in October 1872, the photograph would pre-date Elise and Carl's wedding in 1875 and their departure in 1877.

One interpretation of this photo could be that Catherina sits to the left of her parents, while Elise is on her mother's right. Beside her is Carl, with his hand on her chair as if to link himself organically with the woman of his affections. Immediately behind Elise would be sister Bertha (four years younger). The young woman standing at the extreme right would be the youngest of the Rehder daughters, Maria.

Such photographs were carefully constructed as they would serve as a long-time memento and, in this case, a lasting image to gaze upon for those who left and those who stayed. Kellinghusen was fortunate at the time to have among its residents a well-regarded, long-time early exponent of photographic arts, Detlev Vahlendick, whose work created an extensive record of the town's life and residents.

Like many towns in the German Confederation of the time, Kellinghusen was caught up in the provisioning and servicing for yet another war, this time the Franco-Prussian war of 1870. While the war itself was over in little more than six months, it evoked opposition in Kellinghusen, which had long been a garrison town. On this occasion, the war's greatest impact related to the town's role as a holding place for captured French military personnel. These included soldiers from the French colonies and as confinement in the area was seemingly relaxed, internees had a degree of freedom to move around the town. While the conflict may have brought mixed blessings to Kellinghusen, it did achieve the unification of the German state under Chancellor Otto von Bismarck and the prospect of a period of relative peace.

Another impact of the war related to the repression of those who opposed it. Workers' groups were one such focus of opposition and

Bismarck was quick to label them, and other social democrats, of whom there was a sizeable number in Kellinghusen, as dangerous revolutionaries. The chancellor was keen to restrict their activities. Throughout the 1870s there was growing agitation for workers' rights, universal suffrage and opposition to unemployment, taxes and rising living costs. Such activities were inevitably accompanied by harassment and repression. While typical of many communities throughout Europe at the time, it is possible that the general backdrop of these troubles was a factor in the decision made by Elise and Carl to emigrate to Queensland, part of the great southern continent and many miles from such strife.

One can only speculate as to the real driving forces for that decision, profound as it would be for all concerned. Perhaps Carl and Elise shared a desire to move away from their war-torn town and lives. Perhaps they were just adventurous spirits. Perhaps Carl had been involved in the workers' organisation and felt the need to seek a faraway haven for his young family. We will never know. There is the hint, however, that others in the family harboured some worries about the move and perhaps feared for those taking such an adventurous path.

It is likely the decision that older sister Catherina would accompany the group was a way of easing some of the disquiet and concern. Catherina had lived a relatively independent life for the times. She worked in Hamburg as a lady's maid, a role that seemingly gave her some entrée into a different, more privileged world. She was a mature and composed woman. Then again, maybe Catherina reflected on her own status at 31 years of age and thought that she had more to gain by going into the unknown than staying either at Kellinghusen or Hamburg.

On the other side of the earth, authorities in the recently proclaimed independent colony of Queensland saw the increasing social unrest in Europe as an opportunity to attract suitable migrants. Particular attention was given to those centres in the north of the German states and in Scandinavia as potential sources of migrants to try their luck amidst the opportunities of the Queensland colony. At this time, the port of Hamburg had become one of the great trading posts in humanity, as people flocked to the new world. In most cases that meant America, but Australia also came to figure prominently in that trade. The Rehder family was familiar with Hamburg, but this was to be a new experience as they entered the highly organised emigration process that despatched its human cargo with enormous efficiency. However optimistic may have been the aspirations and hopes, this was serious business.

5

A very difficult passage

On 5 April 1877, Elise and Carl Bresler, with baby son Paul and Catherina Rehder, began their exit from 'the overcrowded market of Europe'. The process for embarkation through the port of Hamburg was extremely well organised. Passengers for the various vessels assembled on shore two or three days before scheduled departure. They were grouped in vessel complements and accommodated in designated areas, to allow the necessary medical checks and other formalities to take place in an orderly way. It was a very deliberate process, rigorous and regimented. In part, the thoroughness of the process was prompted by the sheer numbers of people to be handled. The process involved close coordination between the shipping companies, the German authorities and the port officials.

The Hamburg passenger lists were compiled with great care by the shipping companies. These records indicate that 40,000 people emigrated to Australasia between 1850 and 1879. Direct ship passages from Hamburg to Queensland began soon after the appointment of William Kirchner as emigration agent to Germany in 1870. At that time and as a consequence of the Franco-Prussian war, Prussian authorities prohibited the transportation of German emigrants via English ports. For a time, there were also restrictions on males aged between six and 40 leaving Germany.

Such matters had been resolved by 1877, but health and general provisioning were ongoing concerns for ships embarking from Hamburg on the migration trade. Earlier in 1873 the Queensland government had suspended the migration program from Germany. The official reason was concern about the unsanitary conditions on board many of the vessels, but this was only part of the story, as the high costs of the program were a significant factor, especially when the young colony lurched between boom and bust. Nonetheless, issues with disease and loss of life due to illness, poor ventilation and the lack of basic sanitation remained persistent problems for voyages departing Hamburg.

One study of the sailing vessels departing from Hamburg for Queensland ports concluded that

> ships that left from Hamburg were inferior to the British ships in terms of decency, discipline, safety, cleanliness, medical attention, water and food. German ships were also typically more crowded and mortality was higher than on the British vessels.

The Bresler/Rehder family would soon come to experience the reality behind this assessment.

On working their way through the pre-embarkation processes, the family may have been pleased to learn that they would be travelling on the *Charles Dickens*, operated by the Hamburg-based Rob M. Sloman & Co. line, with just over 500 other passengers, 172 of whom were children. A ship of 1,328 tons, she had been built in Glasgow in 1859, originally serving as a British steamship named *Danube*, and was later converted to a square-rigged sailing ship. She had been operated by the Sloman line since December 1874. Her dimensions were 75 metres by 10.5 metres by 6.71 square metres. The voyage to Brisbane would be her first, both to that destination and under the command of Captain Bochwoldt.

Carl and Elise, with baby Paul and Catherina Rehder, made their farewells to relatives and friends several days before the scheduled departure date. On entering the tightly managed process, meals and sleeping accommodation were provided for the period leading to actual boarding. There was no opportunity for a colourful dockside departure with ribbons and last-minute shouted messages. Such sentimentality was dispensed with in the interests of efficiency and the need to keep procedures on schedule in such a thriving trade. The party was registered as a family group, Catherina identified as passenger 110, Carl as 111, Elise 112 and baby Paul passenger 113. They were the only passengers to list Kellinghusen as home.

The port of Hamburg is around 110 kilometres from the mouth of the Elbe. As a son of Silesia, Carl may have reflected that the river that was taking him out to open seas and a foreign land, rose from streams in his home province. It had come a long way to that point, but he was bound for a place a lot further still. About halfway along this channel, as the river began to widen, they were within distant sight of Kellinghusen. They lined the starboard railing in the hope of having a final sight of home; perhaps the tower of the church, set prominently on the town's knoll, just might have been visible. A day or so after they passed Cuxhaven, the ship pushed into open seas and 97 days later would arrive in Moreton Bay.

At this point, the family was surrendering itself to the skills of the ship's master, the winds and the vagaries of the health and sanitation routines on board. Disease was a concern requiring constant vigilance. Ever present in their minds also would have been the dangers of storms, icebergs, fire and fever. Part of the embarkation process had included instruction on safety and sanitation requirements. On a well drilled ship, these were strictly enforced.

Embarking passengers were encouraged to take with them ample stocks of materials and fabrics that could be sewn and stitched to create handicrafts and other useful items. The primary motive of such activities was to provide a distraction for both minds and hands, during what otherwise would be long and tedious periods of boredom. Elise and Catherina 'hemstitched pillowcases and sheeting, made under-garments and antimacassars'. They also made lamp mats, which involved elaborate stitching and embroidery, and the uppers for slippers. The latter were made of canvas, with colourful cross-stitch designs and were then passed to the men, who attached them to leather soles.

Elise, Carl and Catherina needed to come to grips quickly with the bunking arrangements and the confronting lack of privacy and the press of humanity around them. They would be with other families with children. Conditions for married couples and children were far from pleasant or comfortable and in no way private. One report by a ship's doctor of a passage as late as 1889 gives some insight into the conditions endured:

> ...it was horrid, and even indecent for decent married people to be herded together like beasts, with no privacy to dress or undress, and where, in the close and stuffy double bunks they slept in, only a thin board separated each couple from another alongside, another below, and another lot end to end. The ventilation was very poor, and in the tropics, with a temperature of 90°, the air was mephitic... The married couple slept in bunches of 16 human beings in two tiers...the very young children slept with their parents and the older children piled in together somehow in other double bunks.

Some experts have claimed that Australia's convicts were assured of a safer passage south than many of the emigrants who followed in the next hundred years. The early transportation system placed considerable importance on safety and health, standards that were less strictly complied with as the trade increased and greater use made of private agents. Both in terms of percentage of ships lost and the number of souls lost per individual journey due to disease and illness, the later emigrants fared worse than did the convicts. Not that such statistics were known at the time to those seeking passage to the new world. However, it is sobering to reflect how strong the urge was to take the risk. The greatest wish of anyone boarding a vessel for the journey would have been for fair weather, sufficient wind to ensure a fast passage and no fierce storms, especially at night.

By the 1870s, virtually all shipping lines had adopted the great circle route for journeys to Australia. This involved driving further west down the coast of Africa and then, significantly, much further south into the Southern Ocean and riding its winds and currents for 4,000 kilometres. Ships heading directly for Sydney or Brisbane would continue at this trajectory until sighting Tasmania, when they would haul to the north and head up the east coast of Tasmania and the mainland. Significant savings in time were achieved by this route, but it required a far greater degree of skill on the part of the master and his crew and, depending on the time of year, presented very real dangers from icebergs, raging storms and sheer cold. An April departure meant they could navigate the Elbe without the worst of the winter ice, but would confront the Southern Ocean in all its wintery wildness.

While all this lay ahead of the *Charles Dickens*, the first part of the journey took them along the English Channel, west of Portugal, down the north-west coast of Africa and across the equator. This part of the journey held its own dangers, largely related to the heat and windless conditions. In the crowded shipboard conditions, the still and foetid air was ripe for fevers and respiratory illnesses. In such conditions, the health of even the most robust could be compromised. Babies and young children were at greatest risk of contracting disease and other conditions that could quickly make their health precarious.

As they approached the equator, conditions in the lower decks must have become unbearable. The ship's log records that on 8 May 1877, three days before crossing the equator, a passenger was overcome by the conditions, jumped overboard and drowned. On the same day, nine-month-old Paul Bresler died, seemingly of respiratory problems. The cause of death is recorded simply as bronchitis.

One can only imagine the grief and sadness that would have engulfed Elise and Carl at this development. Some sense of the pain can be glimpsed from one diary entry of a passenger on a later journey:

> I was awakened this morning by a poor woman laying her trembling hand on my shoulder saying 'will you come M'am my baby is dead'. I went with her and prepared the little one for its

watery grave. She bore up bravely but broke down terribly after the funeral…'

Funerals at sea involved a minimum of procedure and ceremony. Usually the body was wrapped in canvas, the occasion full of desolation. An eyewitness to one burial at sea reported that

> …whilst the service was being read, her remains were lowered into the sea which was raging at the time most furiously… It was hard to part from her and to dispose of her remains in this way, but it was necessary to do so, and it matters not where the body is we trust her gentle spirit is in heaven…

In this case, the languid conditions at the time would have made the disposal of the body of a small child a drawn-out, painful process. Rather than the ship moving on swiftly, it would have lingered, perhaps becalmed, bringing adding poignancy, prompting feelings of guilt competing with grief. Life on the seas seemed more fragile than normal. Even the life that stirred in Elise's womb was at risk. She would want to remain a mother.

Whatever else was to happen on this journey, for Elise it would live in her mind as the time she lost her child. Had they not ventured on this journey, Paul would still be alive. This young smiling life, that had once manifested their love, now lived in their hearts as the unbearable cost of their decision to seek a new life in Australia. It would not have been surprising if their remorse led them to remonstrate with themselves and each other. But there was no turning back. Each day brought the inevitable seaboard drama and indignity. Each day their view of the world was engulfed in a ubiquitous sea that stretched to the horizon, tormenting them further and reminding them that as well as possessing their son, it also possessed power over their own lives.

Elise and Carl no doubt wanted the journey to be over. The *Charles Dickens* was now driving due south, closer to the coast of South America than to Africa. They drew a perverse satisfaction as the winds blew stronger and the ship's pace increased. Captain Bochwoldt would have examined his charts and assessed the highest degree of southern longitude he might prudently reach to optimise the powerful force of the westerly winds to speed them across the Southern Ocean. That judgement involved taking into account the season of the year, the state of the ship, the capability of his crew and the well-being of passengers.

After crossing the Tropic of Capricorn, conditions became increasingly colder and instead of foetid equatorial lassitude, passengers were forced to huddle together for warmth, especially as by now they were confronting the southern winter, with its raging winds, huge seas and icy Antarctic blasts.

The inherent nature of the Southern Ocean at this time of year meant that storms and wild winds would be commonplace. The winds were a given, the storms a matter of chance and fate. Large seas would result in waves breaking over the ship and flushing torrents of cold water over the passengers below. Combined with the fury and noise of the storm, the conditions were often terrifying, particularly at night. During one such raging blow, Elise was hit by a barrel that had come loose and she was thrown down a companionway. She was badly injured, having broken a hip. Devastating as that injury was, she was further assailed in a most cruel way when her baby miscarried.

The loss of two children on the voyage south was a crippling burden to bear. Ellen McConachie, who endured a similar fate on a voyage in 1882 wrote in her diary several years later,

> Even yet I yearn after my little ones, but I am content now to wait for the time 'When I no more am drifted upon this surging tide, but with them, safely home upon the other side.' But I do not think this content would ever have been mine had no other little ones come to somewhat fill the aching void. Dear little ones. I should not mind being as they are tonight. For what is our life? A vapour?... I just feel as if after all I had lived in vain.

As was recalled later in a poignant second-hand account,

> ...there was nothing on earth so sad as seeing a body committed

to the deep, and the ship just quietly moving onward to its destination…she [Elise] was a very timid, little person and…she never really could forget those wee ones and their watery grave…

Once again, Elise faced the agonising ritual of disposing of a child's body to the mercies of the sea. On this occasion, the deep ultramarine waters of the Southern Ocean would draw her parcel of unrealised love to its black-ink depths. Only this time she was suffering physical injury as well, which would leave her with lifetime legacies of a limp, limited movement and pain. Elise was confined to bed and rest, however possible, for the remainder of the journey. In such circumstances, she was reliant on the skill and manner of the ship's surgeon, Dr Uterhardt, and his attending matron, Mrs Croucher.

The role of the surgeon involved more than simply ministering to those who became unwell. The office was as responsible as the ship's master for bringing emigrants safely to their destination. Before embarkation, the surgeon examined each passenger. Those considered unwell were not allowed to board.

> Overall their most important function was to be champion and protector of their charges, to care for the weak and to discipline those who were troublesome to others, to demand the best possible diet and treatment from masters. They needed as much skill in human relations as they did in medicine.

Dr Uterhardt would need to invest special care and effort to ensure Elise's health and comfort for the rest of the voyage.

Elise's husband Carl and her sister, Catherina, while bearing their own sense of bereavement, must have held grave fears for Elise and where this disastrous venture was taking her. Certainly by this stage she would have been deeply depressed – melancholic, as it was termed at the time. Healing her fractures would take time and was not helped by the constant and unpredictable movement of the ship. Restoring her equilibrium and attitude would be a task for a longer time. The end of the journey no doubt could not come soon enough, but neither would it come easily. The vessel was afflicted with fevers and illnesses, notably measles, which was particularly prevalent among the children.

On 1 July 1877, the crew sighted Tasmania, a sign that soon they would change course and veer northwards up the eastern coast of their new homeland. Every degree north took them into warmer waters and air. Just as they farewelled their homeland on the starboard side, they could now from time to time glimpse their new homeland on the port side. Given the time of year, before sighting land they may first have smelt it on the breeze. As one similar traveller recorded,

> … Come on deck, and smell the land! People could not at first believe it; but there it was, strong and delicious…the wind is blowing strong off the shore; and the fragrance continues, something like the scent of a hayfield, but more spicy. I expect it is the yellow mimosa [wattle], which my brother Richard said we should now find in flower all over the valleys…

The spirits of both passengers and crew lifted appreciably as they progressed up the coast, coupled with an impatience to be done with the rolling of the sea and the hideously cramped conditions. Their destination – Moreton Bay, doorway to Brisbane, capital of the colony of Queensland – might once have seemed a long way away. Now, although closer, it still seemed a long way away. For Elise, Carl and Catherina, it couldn't come soon enough. The question in their minds was could the fortunes of this new land erase the trauma and tragedy of the past four months? They would be able to regain their land legs, escape the privations of ship life and try to put an end to the suffering. Most importantly they would be able to start the next phase of their lives, the reason why they had embarked on this journey in the first place. Carl, Elise and Catherina cut a sad and stoic image waiting on deck as the *Charles Dickens* entered the safe haven of Moreton Bay.

6

So who are George and Elise?

In their separate journeys, Elise and George began to negotiate one of life's greatest transitions, one in which adaptation and resilience engage in a dance of survival. The urge to hang onto the old and familiar works in tandem with the pull of new experiences and challenges. Sometimes the pull of the familiar leads the dance. At other times it is the challenge of the new. The need is to find a synthesis of difference and continuity. For the emigrant, such elements play out in dramatic form, sometimes involving a great struggle to maintain equilibrium. The need for resolution and its search are often painful and conflicting – a measure of the enormous courage required to embark on the journey of migration.

For the individual emigrant, whether of the 1800s or the early 2000s, there is a kind of dialogue of the self, in which identity evolves and shifts. In this process, memory competes with new realities. There is a need to make sense of things that appear innately strange, if not bewildering. All of these challenges and more confronted Elise and George on their passages from an old to a new world. As George and Elise set off from their respective embarkation ports, London and Hamburg, what sense of themselves did they have? In all likelihood they reflected the circumstances of their lives up to that point and the social conditions in which they were immersed.

George was assured and clear, notwithstanding the unknowns of the future on which he had embarked. He was an Englishman, a man of Shropshire, but pre-eminently a man of the British Empire, setting sail for other parts of that Empire. This journey was his decision and his alone. Elise may have been less confident. She had been raised a member of the Rehder family, but was now known as Bresler, assuming the name and some of the identity of her young husband. Just as her name had changed, so had her nationality, perhaps back and forth, during the wars that had ravaged her home in the 29 years of her life. The immediate considerations on her mind would have been for the care of an infant son throughout the inevitable storms and ravages of the journey. Increasingly she would have been aware of another life stirring in her womb. She would no doubt have taken comfort from the strong support provided by her husband and sister.

But identity has many layers. Some are laid down long before birth. Genetics and family circumstances, social status and conditions have already determined, or at least influenced, much of a child's future prospects. The intersection of chance and fate, so often critical to the choice of life partners, or the union of egg and sperm and its resulting genetic formulation provide a capricious basis for life's journey. Chance and fate can have significant influence on family and social environments, which in turn shape the opportunities and circumstances in which the person develops.

Such considerations are very much 21st-century constructs, accepted as empirical scientific knowledge, but nonetheless useful when contemplating 19th-century lives. Certainly the differences in geographic, environmental and social conditions between Shropshire, Schleswig-Holstein and colonial Queensland were vast, and yet the same basic human aspirations and life strategies applied. To be human is to be human, no matter where the location. But clearly there were differences in the environmental and cultural influences of the Shropshire lad and the Schleswig-Holstein woman, and indeed the Queensland of Terra Australis. Such differences can shape how an individual views the world and responds to its challenges. Understanding that process in the context of a 19th-century world is part of the mystery to be unravelled.

In the case of Elise and George, the lived experiences of their earlier northern hemisphere lives were no doubt shaped by all of the factors referred to above. But in broad terms, family/community, place and nationality loom as key factors in their development and growth. They certainly provide a useful way into understanding the mindsets they would have brought with them to Moreton Bay.

While much was invisibly determined at the times of their birth, George and Elise had learned and absorbed a great deal from the families around them. Routines and rhythms of parental and family life would have laid down patterns of behaviours, based on tradition, expectations and judgements formed by life values and experiences. Overlaid on this were community influences and customs, not just of actions but also of thinking. Such influences could shape the young adult in their development and influence their behaviour, even beyond the time that they set off on a more independent course in life.

Beyond these people-related influences there was also the impact of place – the physical environment and setting in which they lived their lives. Characteristics such as the slope of the horizon, the refraction of the light, the colour of the sky and the productivity of the soil, all have influence. The physical landscape does not just provide the setting and backdrop to our lives, it impacts us directly and can shape who we are and who we become. While often imperceptible and beyond our control, such effects form attitudes and shape mentalities and in so doing fashion thinking and direct minds.

Such influences on young Shropshire and Schleswig-Holstein minds can only be glimpsed by understanding the circumstances and contexts of the time. That such factors have had a considerable influence on the Australian psyche has long been acknowledged. Henry Lawson, at the end of his bizarre tale of 'The Bush Undertaker', drew the challenging conclusion in its final words:

> And the sun set again on the grand Australian bush, the nurse and tutor of eccentric minds, the home of the weird.

Such was the environment that awaited George and Elise – the context into which they brought their own mindsets and mental frames.

All such factors combine to give identity a malleable and fluid quality. It is certainly not fixed in stone, or even flesh and blood. But neither is it capricious. Rather it is shaped and then refashioned by a range of influences. It has its own ambiguities and sometimes conceals its own contradictions, essentially because it is passively fluid and occasionally dynamic. In many ways, it is a state of mind or a disposition that evolves, depending on the events and stimuli encountered. Identity is in part a process of managing interactions and their impacts, of making sense of things and seeking patterns, rhythms and reassurance in what might otherwise appear strange and foreboding. For the emigrant, it is a form of constant negotiation. Elise had more negotiating to do than did George. For her, there was more that was confounding, language and culture being just two.

Although a quiet, gentle and reserved woman, the young Elise appears to have been resourceful and knew her mind. She had seemingly prevailed in the face of family concern about the proposed journey south. She possessed an inner strength. Her perspective on national identity appears to have been one influenced more by her sense of place than any passionate commitment to a nation state. She was a young woman of what was now the Prussian German lowlands, a young woman of Holstein, not driven by a visceral commitment to Germanic culture. She was pragmatic rather than ardent in her nationalism. Prussia had ended the war that had afflicted her life, so she was happy to be Prussian-German. But it was the safety and security of her family that more than any other factor influenced her interest and commitment to the nation state.

Just as Charles Darwin saw individual species as plastic or capable of being shaped and fashioned, so the emigrant needs a capacity to adjust to the ambiguity of an identity that is being shaped and fashioned by their circumstances. For George, the challenge and need for such adaptation was less pronounced than the imperative that Elise would confront. For Elise, the principal focus would be on family, community and place.

7

Quarantine and other trials

There was great excitement on board as the *Charles Dickens* plied slowly into Moreton Bay and the mouth of the Brisbane River, on the morning of Saturday 14 July 1877. Much preparation had preceded the day as passengers gathered and repacked their possessions. Conversations took on a hurried and animated tone as passengers reassured each other that the anxiety of the voyage was at last behind them and they could now concentrate on the business of discovering and learning about their new homeland. Sightings of buildings and activities on the shoreline attracted much comment. Everything was new. It was the new world, at last.

But Captain Bochwoldt and Surgeon Uterhardt had other concerns on their minds. There had been much sickness on the voyage, resulting in 17 deaths. The ship had embarked with 510 passengers but now was disembarking 498 – five births reconciling the ledger. But for Elise those numbers didn't tell the full story. The diseases on board had included measles and typhoid fever. To make matters worse, some on board remained ill, seriously ill. Both men realised that it was unlikely they would be granted pratique by the local shipping authorities. Without this clearance, the ship would not be able to enter port.

The ship anchored in the bay for several days, to facilitate the necessary communications with the port authorities, before clearance to berth. The *Brisbane Courier* reported on 18 July that there had been significant illness and disease on the ship's journey, with children accounting for all but two of the deaths. The report added,

Neither is any reason given for the occurrence of so much sickness; but the number of children on board at the date of sailing was 172, which may be considered far too large a number of children for one vessel.

The following day, captain, crew and passengers confronted the reality of being refused pratique – the *Charles Dickens* was ordered to fly the yellow jack and towed by the government tender *Kate* to a mooring off Peel Island, the colony's quarantine station. The presence of typhoid fever on board was a major concern for local health authorities. The Peel Island facility was the colony's principal line of defence against the importation of disease and epidemics that travelled with new settlers from the old world.

Located on the western side of North Stradbroke Island, Peel Island was largely protected from the swells and blows from the east and the south. The island is broadly rectangular, being roughly five kilometres by two. Its southern foreshore features a broad expanse of sandy beach. Mangroves dominate the shorelines on the western and northern sides. The quarantine station had been built on a bluff on the south-east corner. It had received its first ship in 1873 and a further 23 ships would be directed there throughout the course of that decade. The number increased to 31 in the 1880s, gradually declining to only three in the last decade of the century. The facilities were elementary, consisting of only three buildings, a female ward capable of accommodating 100, a small hospital and another building which served as both a dispensary and storeroom. All cooking was done outdoors. So also, it seems, was the makeshift accommodation for males.

The proper functioning of this short-term community became the responsibility of the surgeon, in whom was vested responsibility for the welfare of passengers. Standard practice was for all passengers and their luggage to be removed from the ship. All of the ship's fittings were stripped out, taken ashore and burned. During the period in quarantine 'linen and clothing was washed and boiled numerous times. The ship was fumigated and refitted with new equipment.'

Such a regime required considerable organisation on the part of Surgeon Uterhardt and disciplined effort by all able-bodied persons. It was a time of great frustration for all. They were within sight of their destination but unable to reach it and get on with the business of forging a new life. Disappointment and frustration abounded but then in addition they were all forced to undertake a seemingly relentless routine of sanitising and washing individual items of luggage and other shared items. The one comfort was that they no longer felt the fluid sway of the sea beneath them and were able to regain their land legs. For Elise Bresler, however, that was easier said than done.

Despite her injuries, Elise is unlikely to have been accommodated in the hospital wing, as that was reserved for those patients ill with the diseases that prompted their quarantine. There was good reason for Elise to be kept separate, lest she succumb to their infections. During the course of the seven weeks on the island, a further six passengers died of their ailments, adding to the pain and pathos of the stay. Those who died were at least afforded a burial on shore, in a small area about 600 metres from the main facilities. In 1877, Peel Island was already the last resting place of 10 others who had journeyed on earlier ships from German ports, only to be ordered to quarantine on arrival.

The inconvenience of being quarantined on the island was not just an affliction borne by the passengers. The crew of the *Charles Dickens* also resented the imposition, as it meant considerable additional work and delay in receiving full payment for their services. For four of the crew, it was an ordeal they decided they could and would avoid. Some days after mooring off Peel Island, four sailors abandoned the small community and used a ship's rowboat to go ashore in Brisbane. Absconding from quarantine was considered a serious matter by health authorities, as it risked the spread of highly contagious diseases in the community.

Local police made the capture of the offenders a high priority. On the morning of 1 August 1877, Swedish sailor Charles Larss appeared in the Water Police Court charged with deserting from the ship *Charles*

Dickens on 29 July, larceny of a lifeboat from the ship and escaping from the quarantine station in Moreton Bay. Later the same day, his co-conspirators and fellow Swedes, Siren Jensen, Julius Larsen and Jacob Olsen faced similar charges. All were remanded in custody.

The four appeared again in court on 10 August and pleaded guilty to a single charge of 'Leaving and going onshore from the *Charles Dickens* then in quarantine on 29 July 1877.' This single charge, and the dropping of the charge of larceny relating to the lifeboat, appeared to indicate a less punitive approach by the authorities. The penalty applied, however, offered no comfort for the offenders as the magistrate's sentence was 'six months imprisonment and to pay a fine of £150 [each], in default, to be imprisoned for a further period of six months'. In all likelihood, the four sailors faced spending a year in prison. The case attracted much attention in the Brisbane community with claims that the sentence was too harsh, leading to a petition to the Governor for mercy.

Those who remained on Peel Island were probably unaware of the consequences facing the four absconders. From their perspective there were simply four less able-bodied men to undertake the tasks required to prepare the ship, its passengers and their luggage to a condition that would enable them all to obtain clearance from the health authorities. While much of the time on the island would have been spent in the outdoors, the climate and weather conditions of Brisbane in August were pleasantly mild, with average daily temperatures around 21 to 23 degrees Celsius.

The mild temperatures, sunshine and steady ground underfoot would have been appreciated by Elise and an aid to her healing. However, the time in quarantine would mean that any access to further medical attention was delayed and effectively denied. Elise's hip would mend in its broken state. Her limp would be permanent, her pain and discomfort lifelong. Life in their new land would now be more difficult and challenging. These were but thoughts and worries as the party of three endured the final days of quarantine and began to contemplate life in Brisbane town.

Following final clearance to disembark, groups of passengers and their luggage were transported on the *Kate* to the Brisbane docks early in the second week of September. From there they were taken to the immigration depot, which would provide lodgings for a short period, serve as a clearing house for those seeking work and accommodation, and generally provide the support and information that new settlers required.

At this point, Elise, Carl and Catherina stepped into a lacuna of emigrant life. Little is known of their circumstances in those early years of emigrant settlement. It is assumed that Catherina continued to live with Carl and Elise in the short term. Her practical assistance would have been particularly valuable in the early months. However, she would need to find her own employment and, given her work experience, that could have involved leaving Brisbane. It is likely, however, that a key strategy of the group initially would have been to build contacts with the Schleswig-Holstein community and through that network acquire work and accommodation. Carl would no doubt be looking for an opportunity in the tailoring field – a notice in the *Brisbane Directory* around that time of a tailor, Chas. Bresler in Spring Hill, suggests that he may have had a degree of success.

The bare facts of what we do know with certainty derive from a series of official documents, each of which tells its own story. In July 1878, William Max was born to Elise and Carl. On 8 November 1878, young William died of congestion of the brain, seemingly a fever that had raged for several days. The family were living at Kangaroo Point at the time. Then on 4 December 1880, Carl Bresler died at Vulture Street, South Brisbane. The cause of death is stated as phthesis (TB) and pulmonary congestion, a condition from which he had suffered for two of the three years that he had spent in the colony. His death certificate stated starkly that he had fathered three children – all males and all dead.

It is hard to contemplate the range of emotions that must have accompanied each of these events. The birth of another child would have been an occasion of great joy. At last their family was restored. Elise was once again a mother; perhaps now some of the pain of the earlier loss of the two on the voyage could be assuaged. The loss of this third child, however, would have been such a cruel blow and the source of great grief and sadness. It would have plunged both parents into severe depression, reminding them of all the futility and pain that had descended on their world since setting off from Hamburg in April 1877.

Painful as the loss of her third child would have been for Elise, it is likely that nothing would have prepared her for the blow of Carl's death. Now, definitively, her world was sundered. She no longer had someone else which whom to endure the pain. Her life would have appeared pointless, futile. The disasters that had followed their brave decision to seek a better life in the new world now mocked that life itself. Elise had learned to endure and overcome much in the past three years, but the loss of Carl severed a large part of her life source. She had never been an overtly confident and outgoing woman, rather someone with her own inner strength, who drew on the energies and aspirations of those closest to her. Carl, who had enveloped her in his youthful enthusiasms, was now no longer at her side. She was 33 years old and alone. Life's vagaries had seemingly rejected her motherhood, disabled her bodily frame and now deprived her of her life partner and solace. This journey of adventure to the new world had taken her through a long tunnel of suffering to a place that treated her cruelly. Would it ever end? How might it end? What would she do now? She would need to find the resources within her to survive.

8

Starting to 'butty' in Homestead 4171

Acting on his own advice, Peter Kuskopf moved his family north to Merriman Flat (later Palmwoods) in late 1881 or early 1882. Peter had acquired a stretch of land from a previous landholder. It was a busy household with young baby Anna and Peter's retinue of six sons, the eldest of whom by then was nearing 15. Catherina gave birth to another daughter in the August of 1882. Despite the numbers, they were soon joined by George, his two children Maria and Henry, and Elise as housekeeper. George had in mind to acquire a smaller adjoining lease and, while living with Catherina and Peter, to fell timber on the property and build his own house. These two family groups, along with Momme and Christine Bendixen (Peter Kuskopf's youngest sister), were the original settlers in what became the township of Palmwoods.

In December 1883, George submitted a formal application to become the lessee of 160 acres of Crown land at an annual rent of £4. In the official records, the selection became known as Homestead/Selection 4171. Seemingly, George had trouble with the bureaucracy of the day, as in March 1885 he wrote to the Under Secretary Public Lands advising that he had now been residing on the land for 14 months and had made numerous improvements but had not received confirmation of his lease arrangements. His neighbours had received confirmation of their notices and had urged him to pursue the matter. Such confirmation was subsequently recorded on 21 July 1885. However, there was a further complication a year or two later which put George's tenure at risk. He learned that an agent in South Brisbane, to whom he had entrusted the money to make the annual rent payments, had not done so and a formal Reversal of Forfeiture needed to be issued in May 1887, following payment of the outstanding monies.

An inspection of the selection carried out on behalf of the Department of Public Lands in January 1889 revealed that the residence on the property was a four-room slab house with a gabled shingle roof. The house was valued at £40, yards and outbuilding were valued at £10, and fencing and railings at £43/10/-. In addition, the report indicates that 20 acres had been felled and cleared, six acres stumped and ploughed, and three acres planted with fruit and other crops that included coffee, ginger, maize and potatoes. The total value of the improvements was estimated at £286/10/- and formed the basis of the formal issue of a Deed of Grant of the land to George Fewtrell in April 1889.

The land held by George was subsequently reduced by two excisions to facilitate the construction of the main road north to Gympie and the railway. The route for the railway had been planned initially to take a different line but in the end cut through the Fewtrell property, a change prompted by the ready supply of water for steam engines, available from a nearby lagoon. George received small payments in compensation for the losses arising from these developments, for both of which he was a keen advocate. In the years immediately before his departure from Shropshire, George became well aware of the developmental impact of the extension of the railway. He had reason to think it would not be any different in Queensland. He was keen to play his part in the opening up of the area and the building of facilities that would enhance the capacity to take his own produce to the Brisbane market and beyond. The proximity of the railway station and freight loading facility to the Fewtrell orchard, a short walk from the homestead, proved to be of great convenience and, in time, economic benefit.

It was probably sometime in 1882 that the 'understanding' between

Elise and George changed. As with many frontier relationships at the time, circumstances brought people together in situations where companionship led to a de facto husband and wife arrangement. Such unions were common, both in colonial settings and, as George would have been aware, in Shropshire. In fact, there was a term for the arrangement in the common parlance of Shropshire at the time – 'to butty'. This was a domestic application of a usage that originally referred to the custom in English collieries of working in pairs. Life in the Australian bush was driven by common human needs and demanded practical solutions.

George and Elise were no doubt drawn together by a sense of shared common misfortune. In simple terms, they needed each other and came to realise that being together as husband and wife offered them both the opportunity for a second chance to forge a secure future and realise their aspirations. Conscious that the completion and move to the new home inevitably would bring sharper public focus on their domestic arrangements, George and Elise decided to invest in the mutual respect they shared. Both were Protestants. They married at the Registry Office in Brisbane on 13 April 1883. They could grow to love each other after, rather than before, marriage – not unusual for the times.

The wedding took place on a Friday, probably chosen at the time for reasons of convenience. Friday the 13th it may have been but at least it was not a Wednesday or Saturday – in Shropshire folklore and superstition, such days were considered inauspicious for weddings. It was said that weddings on Wednesday foreshadowed a life of poverty, while a Saturday marriage could lead to an early death. It is not known if George was a superstitious man, swayed by such beliefs, although he may have reflected that his marriage to Maria Taylor had been on a Saturday! On this occasion, however, the prospects were auspicious and on 14 February 1884, Elise once again became a mother. As if to confirm that things were now different, she had a daughter, Annie.

One could imagine that Elise would have had mixed feelings at the thought of bringing another child into the world. She had experienced over and again the pain of losing a young baby. Part of her must have feared a repeat of those earlier sadnesses. Nevertheless, she had now a further, perhaps unexpected, chance to raise her own. Whatever the doubts, whatever the fears, things were different now and she must look forward. This was her season and the family's first decade in the area was one of fecundity and consolidation. Notwithstanding the difficulties and risks, Elise gave birth to three more children – Emma, a second daughter, in March 1886;, George James in June 1888; and a second son, Samuel Markus, in March 1891, who was given the names of each of his male grandparents. At the time of Sam's birth, George was 47 years old and Elise was 43.

The two children from George's first marriage, Maria and Henry, were by now in their early teenage years and inevitably played important roles in assisting with the running of what became a very busy frontier household. Catherina also delivered four children to Peter Kuskopf, three daughters and a son. Catherina came to have much experience of childbirth, serving as a midwife in the area for many years. It is hard to imagine that she would not have attended the births of Elise's four children born at Palmwoods, especially given the complications that could have arisen.

The young community at Palmwoods, while small, was tight-knit, relatively isolated and focused on the twin challenges of family and mastering the land. As such, it was a typical Queensland frontier community. The fact that the early settler families all shared a German (Schleswig-Holstein) heritage was not of itself unusual, as at that time nine per cent of immigrants to Queensland were German-born. The Queensland colony overall was now experiencing the impact of the ardent emigrant drives of earlier decades. One such outcome was the growing diversity in the population's background and an early significant dilution of the percentage of British stock. By 1891 a third of the German emigrants to Australia resided in Queensland. It was not until 1901 that the majority of the colony's population was born in Queensland. Clearly it was not just in Palmwoods that the earlier waves of newcomers were busy growing their families.

While in some parts of Queensland the German community tended to aggregate in more isolated communities, the mix in Palmwoods ensured that there was a different focus. This was due partly to geography – Palmwoods was on the road and the railway to somewhere (mostly Gympie and beyond) – and to the mix of backgrounds and the openness of the settler group.

Certainly George Fewtrell was British and now part of a broader Schleswig-Holstein network. His activities and his associations with the pioneering dynamo Peter Kuskopf were very much focused on developing the area as a productive part of the broader community. Kuskopf was at this time moving into his latest and last business venture, a butcher's shop in Woombye, returning to a trade he had learned from his father in his homeland. Always one to see an opportunity, this time he planned to raise the cattle himself in nearby paddocks, before slaughter and sale at the shop.

During the 1880s and early 1890s, Queensland was afflicted with major natural disasters and significant financial difficulties. In 1886–88 the western areas of the colony were in severe drought. In January and February 1887, there was major cyclone activity on the coast, resulting in extensive flooding from Bundaberg to Brisbane. Other cyclones visited the area in March 1890, April 1892 and February 1893. Brisbane experienced two very large floods in the space of only a few weeks in 1893. Bank failures and parlous government finances heralded a severe recession in the 1890s.

It was during these times that the ethos of the yeoman farmer began to pay dividends in the emergence of small productive, agriculturally based settlements and communities. A key priority had been to diversify the Queensland economy from the dominance of pastoralism and a fixation on the exaggerated and speculative potential of gold. What was happening among the hillsides of Palmwoods and Woombye was the very type of development, both economic and social, that had been championed by Griffith's liberals and key republicans. Their focus had been to push back the power of the pastoralists, encourage closer settlements of farmers and broaden the base of the colony's economy. Allied to these goals was an emphasis on opportunities for the egalitarian sharing of the fortunes of the colony.

This was the type of hands-on Empire building for which George Fewtrell had signed on. He was now busily involved in growing his family, as well as the farming enterprise and the community he was helping to establish, in a part of the British Empire named in honour of the same sovereign he knew in Shropshire. He was doing so in company with his wife and her sister and brother-in-law, all of whom were of similar mind, despite being of different European origins. Growing their families and adjusting to the land and its landscape was the context for their endeavours of community building, in what by now was becoming a place that they increasingly identified as home.

9

'This land is mine: this land is me'

When George and Elise first travelled north to Palmwoods, in all probability they did so by coach. Services were irregular but the alternative was a sea journey and then overland from the river estuaries. In November 1868, Cobb & Co. established a service from Brisbane to Gympie, with a halfway stop at Woombye, one of a series of depots along the way. Whatever way they journeyed, Elise and George could not have failed to see the striking outline of the Glass House Mountains, the highest peak rising to 556 metres above the surrounding landscape. Elise would have found such sharp and arresting features, emerging from the broad coastal plain, quite different to any horizon she may have gazed upon in the low lands of Schleswig-Holstein. George might have reflected that these were far more dramatic place markers of his new territory, than was the Wrekin in Shropshire. In truth, they travelled through and settled in the remnant caldera of an ancient volcano. They were not the first, just the latest, to ponder the influence of these geographical features.

The deed granting the land for Homestead Selection 4171 was formally issued to George Fewtrell in April 1889, in the name of Victoria, sovereign of 'the United Kingdom of Great Britain and Ireland, Queen, Defender of the faith' and in conformity of the laws 'for the alienation of Crown Lands in Our Colony of Queensland'. It defined the area, consisting of 155 acres, one rood and 21 perches, as precise lines drawn at geometric angles and extending to and from measured distances from specific reference points. The document said the property was in the County of Canning and the Parish of Mooloolah. It was British administration at its clearest. This was the space designated as home for George and his family. But for all its precise clarity, it was an artificial construct drawn up in accordance with the Crown Lands Alienation Act of 1876. It was a marker of the *terra nullius* world view that prevailed. Although well-intended, it was ultimately flawed as a descriptor of place and ownership. It was land possessed and used by others – land that 'was in fact seething with an ancient rhythm'.

The families Kuskopf, Fewtrell and Bendixon were not the first people to live in these parts. Nor were they even the first white people to frequent the area. Its occupation by Aboriginal people stretched back thousands of years, and since the 1820s there had been early waves of white incursion. Initially this was in the form of escaped convicts fleeing the Moreton Bay penitentiary, an early and unsuccessful push by a few pastoralists in the 1850s and then an influx of timber-getters in the 1860s and 1870s.

Before and throughout all these years, the Aboriginal peoples of the Sunshine Coast area had heard stories of the inexorable advance of the white man. They were not unprepared for the contact, both first and ongoing. Those preparations included resistance and accommodation, but ended ultimately in dispossession and removal. The violence and tragedy of the clash between cultures on the Sunshine Coast area and its hinterland was probably similar to that which occurred in many other areas on the Australian landmass. It was marked, however, by a tragic poignancy that has particular relevance to the modern Australian nation of which it was to become part.

The Sunshine Coast is the country of the Gubbi Gubbi people and traditionally comprised several different clans and language groups. Those who lived close to the coast were of the Undanbi language group, those closer to the range formed part of the Nalbo language group. Essentially, the division ran north to south on a line roughly consistent with the northern rail line, which was extended through the area around the turn of the 20th century along what was believed to have been a traditional Aboriginal path. The Nalbo people lived along the eastern slopes of the Blackall Range. There was regular contact and movement between the two groups, taking advantage of seasonal changes in climate and food sources.

The modern-day Palmwoods sits in the lands of the Nalbo people. As it is today, it was a territory traversed regularly in migrations between coast and range. Those movements were part of a cycle that involved wintering from April to September on the warmer, sun-filled coast and river estuaries, moving on to well-watered but shady rainforests and swamp areas inland until December and then spending the hot summer months on the cooler areas of the range. The Nalbo people shared a similar culture with the Dallambara (Dalla) people, whose lands covered the plateau of the range. Both were mountain rainforest people, as was evident in their totems. The name Dalla is from the term in the local language for the staghorn, which flourishes in the rainforest. Nalbo is the name of the gum from pine trees. The western name Palmwoods was historically based on the dense thickets of piccabeen (bangalow) palms that distinguished the area.

Every second or third year, the time spent in the mountains was special as it involved participation, with the neighbouring Dalla people, in the great bunya festival of Baroon. This was centred on the fruiting of the bunya nuts, an event that occurred at irregular intervals, but usually every third year when a bumper crop was produced, in February and March. It was an occasion of major cultural significance and shared with tribal groups from as far north as places now known as Bundaberg and Gayndah, as far south as Narrabri and to the west as far as St George and beyond. Tom Petrie, who as a young man had attended a Bunya festival, stated that around six or seven hundred Aboriginal people attended. It was a sharing and celebration of the bounty of the bunya, not just as a delicacy, but as a totem of great cultural significance – a highly organised and structured event in which the returning tribes gathered at and used only those clusters of Bunya tree that they knew to be allocated to them.

The bunya festivals represented a high point in the cultural and social life of Aboriginal people in the wider district. It was a meeting of different tribal groups, not just to share the bounty of the land, but to also exchange information and stories. It was a festival of feasting, socialising and resting. It involved organised pastimes such as wallaby drives, bunya tree climbing and other team type events, such as wrestling and throwing activities, along with water games of mimicking swans and turtles. It was also the occasion for arranging marriages and addressing issues in dispute between neighbouring groups. In explaining the highly organised and respectful manner in which such festivals were conducted, one early writer made the observation that 'These people set us an example that with all our boasted civilisation we might well follow.'

Tom Petrie later described aspects in his *Reminiscences*:

> The dancers would keep up these gaieties for a couple of hours and then all would return to camp, where they settled down to a sort of meeting somewhat after the style of a Salvation Army gathering. One man would stand up and start a story or lecture of what had happened in his part of the country, speaking in a loud tone of voice, so that all could hear. When he finished, another man from a different tribe stood forth and gave his description, and so on till all the tribes had been represented.

There was a clear political element to these occasions. While the 20 or more tribal groups that attended may have had disagreements and even wars, it is said that the festival provided the opportunity to work together at a higher level. 'All these people recognised a common identity in the Bunya Dreaming.' The heads of various tribes and groups would talk about and report on experiences that they had encountered and take from the gatherings news and knowledge of others. It was in this context that news spread about the impact of the white colonial advance, with re-enactments of attacks of gunfire and the poisoning of water holes. In time, the very failure of some groups to send representatives to bunya festivals told its own stark truth.

Awareness of the significance that the bunya festivals and the area of the Baroon held for local Aboriginal people grew slowly among early white colonials. Although the Baroon was only about 30 kilometres from Palmwoods, it was separated by an escarpment of 100 metres. The intensity with which Aboriginal groups protected the Baroon area from white incursion, became an obvious indicator of the importance they attached to both the Bunya tree and the area itself. Tom Petrie, the son of a senior colonial administrator, who grew up and played with Aboriginal children, came to have a unique insight into the bunya celebrations and their cultural importance. Petrie learned their language and culture and in return earned their respect. He advocated to the then Governor Gipps of the colony of New South Wales that it was imperative the area of the bunya tree be protected.

He had a strong, well placed ally in Christopher Rolleston, Commissioner for Crown Lands for the Darling Downs, who 'recognised the importance of the Bunya Mountains to the Aboriginal people of the future southern Queensland, and recommended that the area be set aside for an Aboriginal reserve'. The motivation of both advocates seems to have been to ensure that Aboriginal people retained lands that were highly significant to them and thereby ensure that they could continue to live in those lands and be sustained by them, both physically and culturally.

Governor Gipps took particular interest in the matter and during an extended visit to Brisbane accepted the advice. In April 1842, the Bunya Proclamation was published in the *NSW Government Gazette* prohibiting the occupation of land within a broad, but loosely defined, area on which bunya trees were known or thought to grow. In effect, the area covered by the proclamation extended from the peaks of the range to the Pacific Ocean and in the north from the Maroochy River to an ill-defined point north of Moreton Bay. It certainly included the yet to be settled area that would come to be known as Palmwoods. For all its imprecision, the proclamation was generally respected in the period up until the separation of Queensland from the colony of

New South Wales in 1859. Legislation regarding Crown lands, passed subsequently by the Queensland colonial government, had the effect of nullifying the Bunya Proclamation. This was followed by extensive timber-felling operations in most areas of the hinterland and ultimately by the Crown Lands Alienation Act of 1876, on which basis George Fewtrell became the owner of Homestead Selection 4171.

While the initial motivation for the Bunya Proclamation was driven by a seemingly genuine concern for the Aboriginal people and a somewhat surprising degree of cultural sensitivity, in practice it seems likely that escalating incidents around the time leading up to its gazettal gave the move added momentum. Certainly it was clear that Aboriginal people had a fierce determination to defend the Baroon area from white incursion. However, the poisoning of a large number of Aboriginals on a property at Kilcoy, to the north of the Bunya Baroon, in January 1842 inflamed the situation. More than 100 years later, this event would be described in a semi-official account as 'the death pudding of arsenic, a trap which took seventy native lives, for the theft of half a bag of flour…'

Leaders of tribes attending the bunya festival of 1842 met within the physical and cultural framework of a Bora council, the highest and most sacred authorisation, and decided to actively cooperate in resisting the white advance. More recent scholarship of the culture and sources of the time interprets the Aboriginal responses as being consistent with cultural law, and the obligations that kinship placed on young men to avenge and exact payback for the deaths of others. Noted Dalla warrior Dundalli provides a case study of how strict and honourable observance of cultural lore and practice could lead to a series of attacks on specific people, homesteads and stock which, while honourable and measured in Aboriginal terms, were perceived by the white community as rampant atrocities.

In chronicling the story of Dundalli, Libby Connors has identified how

> according to Gubbi Gubbi oral history Dundalli was a kooringal – a

man charged with carrying out the instructions of the Bora council. The old men knew the hereditary laws but they required someone of 'conspicuous courage and force of character' to enforce it.

Often this could mean acting as a moderating influence on younger men determined on a more aggressive path. In other instances, it required the killing of specific people and/or stock. This did not relate just to the white community but included, in many instances, representatives of neighbouring clans and tribes.

Dundalli was eventually captured and hung on a public scaffold in Brisbane in January 1855. Certainly the period between 1843 and 1855 is seen by Aboriginal sources as a time of active resistance – a 'Black War' – especially in the area around the Baroon festival grounds. It is worth noting that Cilento's semi-official account of the times, published a century later does not hesitate to call it a 'Black War' that 'flared after the great bunya festivals of 1841 and 1844'. In the 1850s the 'Sunshine Coast was an alien land to the whites'. Resistance, particularly around the Baroon grounds, was fierce until the 1860s. The extent that tribal groups did coordinate their resistance diminished gradually over time, as individual groups were impacted more than others and pushed onto the territory of others, generating intertribal disputes.

Against this background, the activities of the Native Police, now under the direction of Queensland authorities following separation from NSW, caused further alarm among Aboriginal people, particularly in the north of the district. Their role was 'to clear the frontiers of white settlement of troublesome Aboriginals' or to undertake the euphemistically termed task of 'dispersal'. In effect, in most cases this meant killing. Records indicate that they were particularly active in the region in 1861 and 1862. One account records that under its commander Fred Wheeler, the force 'dispersed the 'bunya bunya natives' (presumably the Nalbo and Dallambara of the Nambour-Maleny-Kennilworth region)'. The following year they engaged with 'a grand force of Obi Obi (Maleny – Mapleton), Brisbane and Caboulture warriors' and 'managed to disperse these too'.

Commissioner Rolleston had his own reservations as to the extent the Bunya Proclamation could adequately protect the area. In 1851 he raised his concerns with the Chief Commissioner that 'some white settlers were deliberately destroying bunya-bunya trees in order to try to clear the region of Aboriginal people'. The early push by pastoralists was effectively driven back by the thickness of the vegetation and the impracticality of the landscape for that role. Early timber-getters tended to start from the coastal reaches, from where timber that was logged could be more easily floated out for milling. The progress of both industries was largely thwarted by the geography and its vegetation. The pastoralists withdrew and the timber-getters looked for easier pickings – but not before leaving the district with the stain of Aboriginal massacres.

The most notable of these occurred at the aptly named Murdering Creek, near the south-east corner of Lake Weyba, equidistant from the current-day Noosa Heads and Coolum Beach. Accounts vary somewhat but there is little doubt that the event did take place, either in the 1860s or early 1870s. It involved the luring of a group of Aboriginals into an area from where there was little escape from a barrage of shots. The number killed is said to be 'unknown', but at least one account puts the number at 70 and another reports that subsequently 'the tribe ceased to function as a unit following this event'. The motive for the massacre is attributed to either retribution for cattle spearing or a dispute over land usage.

Another massacre is reported in Aboriginal testimonies as having occurred at Eudlo near Didillibah, a mere five or six kilometres from Palmwoods. This area is heavily timbered country with defined sections of open grasslands that even today bear characteristics that Bill Gammage has catalogued as representative of land that was regularly occupied and productively used by Aboriginal people. This event is believed to have occurred in the 1870s, although there is scant documentary evidence of the details. The position of the Aboriginal people in Palmwoods and surrounding areas declined at an alarming rate as the decade of the 1870s rolled on. Traditional practices and food sources gradually became less readily available. This resulted in displaced members of neighbouring tribes encroaching on areas that traditionally belonged to other groups. The basis of societal structures of the Gubbi Gubbi people had begun to fray.

Ultimately, all Aboriginal people of the area felt the impact of dispossession and removal. This process was well advanced by the time George and Elise took up their selection. It was as if the early incursions of pastoralists and timber-getters, supported by the Native Police and destructive massacres, were the first stage in the clash of civilisations and cultures. This was the 'run them out' part of the equation. The second phase of the process, the 'bring them in' factor, was the issuing of settlement selections under the Crown Lands Alienation Act. It was at this nexus point in the 'run them out and bring them in' policy that George and Elise came to the area. The selectors, yeoman farmers and their families constituted the coming of Western/British civilisation to settle the land and tame the environment, which was then seen to include the now dispossessed Aboriginal people of the Gubbi Gubbi.

By the 1880s the Gubbi Gubbi people were considered part of a race that was inferior and doomed. Ironically, this view was in part built on a crude interpretation of the principle of natural selection that had been outlined by Shropshire's foremost son, Charles Darwin. Now among the wave of new arrivals would be another son of Shropshire, George Fewtrell, who would apply other practical farming principles learned in Shropshire and espoused by Darwin. By this stage, the depravity of 'dispersal' had given way to removal to reserves, such as Cherbourg to the north. It was the policy of the government that the area be settled and any doubters took solace that it was also 'the intent of the Almighty we should cultivate the ground'.

The proud owners and custodians of the Bunya lands had been reduced to straggling groups seeking food and blankets from the homesteads of white settlers. Marie Krebs, daughter of Catherina and Peter Kuskopf and a cousin and neighbour of the Fewtrell children, wrote in 1955 of her recollections of the early 1880s,

These were the days when aborigines roamed the district in groups of 50 to 100. They would seem fearsome to people now, but it was a big part of our life, and we were happy to see them and have their company for a few days.

Tom Petrie would later reflect,

How different a native was in those old times! He was full of manly vigour and energy, his life was a joy to him, and the search for his food one long pastime…the white man is accountable for their deterioration. He taught them to drink and to smoke, and to feel it was not worth calling up sufficient energy to make a canoe, a vessel for water, or even a hut to sleep in.

10

A community emerges

Palmwoods is about 20 kilometres from the coast. It is hinterland country, rolling hills running up to the Blackall Range. From Palmwoods to nearby Montville, perched on the edge of the range, the climb is steep. In the 1890s, transportation was fraught and tracks quickly became impassable in wet conditions. There was little by way of a roadway between Palmwoods and the coast. Most traffic plied the Mooloolah River and the upstream network of creeks. However, it was largely a one-way flow to the coast, as the principal resources of the area since the first incursion of white settlers in the late 1830s were the very large and dense stands of timber, which found their outlet through sawmills near the mouth of the river.

Early attempts to develop a cattle industry foundered after a decade, due largely to the dense vegetation and adverse conditions. The need to clear the land led to an initial focus on the rich and relatively easy pickings of good timber, notwithstanding the almost impenetrable undergrowth of vines and other lush subtropical vegetation. The lure of good stands of red cedar brought many to the area and spawned a voracious industry and trade that lasted for several decades. Other timbers that abounded included white cedar, bunya and hoop pines, mahogany, black bean, flooded gum and turpentine. Today these are recognised as rainforest species and subject to strict logging conditions, but for many years they were felled incessantly in the interests of civilising the landscape. The resulting timber, in many cases, was put to uses that were simply industrial, such as fence posts, barns and fruit boxes. Nevertheless, they provided employment and income and helped to underwrite the growth of the area.

The landscape of much of the hinterland of the now Sunshine Coast is radically different to that which confronted early settlers in the mid to late 1800s. When the Fewtrells, Kuskopfs and Bendixons arrived in Palmwoods to make their own contributions to the work of civilising and cultivating, a good deal of the large timbers had already been taken from the area. Nonetheless, the extent of land clearing was a key criterion for having a lease converted to a grant of land. The rich soil had to be liberated to work its magic on crops and other agricultural production. This was of course the essence of the role of the smallholding yeoman farmer. It was what would feed and support a family and it was what was required to sustain a growing Brisbane and Queensland. It was soil rich in the volcanic residues of the massive remnant crater that ringed much of the coastline and extended back to the range.

In addition to establishing a home and farm, there was the immediate and growing need to arrange schooling for the young children who constituted the bulk of the family and community numbers. Such demands were a critical second stage of the drive for settlement across the colony. The Queensland Education Department had recognised that it would not be able to meet all demands for schools and teachers and introduced a system of provisional schools and official schools. The former were basically a mechanism for delaying the capital cost involved in providing a new school, by requiring the parents or local community to meet most of the costs for an initial period of five years. If, at the end of that period, there was an ongoing requirement with a sustainable number of children attending school, the status of the school could be converted from provisional to official, with a corresponding transfer of the financial responsibility to the department. A key consideration of the department was that many settlements were short-lived, so the mechanism was a means of ensuring that priorities were better assessed and the limited expenditure not squandered.

Much advocacy was required for a school at a settlement the size of Palmwoods to be recognised by the authorities. George Fewtrell and Peter Kuskopf were keenly involved in those efforts, which led to the granting of provisional status to the school in 1889. The first school was built by the community, a simple structure like all in the district. The work continued following the school's opening, with students engaged in the clearing of the grounds and playing area. The school serviced the education needs of children in the area whose families were engaged either in farming or timber-getting. Kuskopf, Bendixen and Fewtrell names figured prominently in the first school roll. While many of the timber families in time moved on, George Fewtrell had a long interest and association with the school, having allocated part of his land for its function. He would sometimes attend the school break-up picnic and distribute prizes to the pupils. In 1905, although no longer a parent with an enrolled child, George was elected to the school committee and subsequently to the role of chair. This was at a time when George seemed to have been active in just about every aspect of community life.

The local community was similarly resourceful in attending to their spiritual needs. Building a church and having it staffed by a minister were two key, but not necessarily related, challenges. George took a particular interest in this project. Initially it was thought that the Church of England would provide a minister for the church. However, when this failed to occur, George approached other denominations and eventually obtained the services of a minister of the Methodist Church. Changing denominations was a practical solution given the circumstances and the times. George later served as a local preacher at the church, conducting services on a rostered basis and organising the Sunday school for instruction of the children. As superintendent of the Sunday school, he was responsible for its organisation and functioning. In 1904 he reported to the church community that there were 36 children on the roll and an average attendance each week of 24, adding '…on the whole satisfactory progress was being made'.

With the coming of the railway and the gradual build-up of agricultural enterprises, the Palmwoods/Woombye area continued to develop during the 1880s, leading to calls for the establishment of a separate local government entity. The area was administered by the Caboolture Divisional Board, but agitation for a local Maroochy council gathered pace. A petition, signed by many in the area, was lodged with the Colonial Secretary's office in early 1890. George Fewtrell and Peter Kuskopf were among those calling for local autonomy and their efforts were successful later that year, with the first meeting of the Maroochy Divisional Board held at Petrie's Creek (now Nambour) on 24 September 1890. The meeting was convened by the local member of the Legislative Assembly, Matthew Battersby (who was to hold the seat of Moreton for a brief 11 months), so that the nine elected members could begin their work by selecting a chairman. In 1891, the population of the district served by the Maroochy Divisional Board was 2,030.

George Fewtrell was among the members elected to the first board, beginning a decade of very active and energetic representation of his local interests and a record that reveals much about the man and his values. George served two periods as chairman of the board, being first appointed to the role in July 1893. His advocacy for the establishment of the board was obviously driven by a clear passion for the development of the area. His interest in issues coming before the board revealed a consistent focus on facilitating that development, as well as protecting the interests of the community. The wording of motions that he put regularly to the board used the formulation 'that the land be thrown open for selection'. He was enthusiastic in pursuing such matters, having the board

George Fewtrell as chairman of the Maroochy Divisional Board. (Photo from the official portrait collection of Maroochy Shire leaders, now held by the Nambour & District Historical Museum.)

Maroochy Divisional Board meeting, 1898.

write to ministers in Brisbane or organise delegations to meet with ministers on issues of concern to the community or the board.

The new local government entity was created at a difficult time. There was considerable dispute at the time between farmers and timber interests concerning the condition of roads in the area. In addition, Queensland governments at the start of the 1890s reduced the funding allocation to local shire boards, seriously limiting their ability to improve amenities at the local level. George was a consistent advocate of creative and innovative approaches to support developments that were in the community interest. A common theme to these ideas was seeking revenues from different sources, combined with innovative ways to ensure that those who benefitted most, bore the largest part of the cost of their provision. These included the seeking of grants and loans from the Queensland government for specific road and bridge projects.

In 1898, George proposed, with unanimous support, that an application be made to the Treasurer of Queensland for a loan of £400 for development of the Hunchy to Palmwoods road, and that 'a special or separate rate be given over the area benefitted thereby'. George was also

George's signature on a Maroochy Divisional Board document. (From documents held at the Maroochy Shire archive.)

successful in urging the board to insist that 'Wheel Licence' fees be paid, on the basis that all such fees paid should be allocated to expenditure 'on the roads where collected'. In these instances, George was an early advocate of the user pays principle and the hypothecation of revenues.

It would seem that George was driven by a clear moral compass, based on the individual making a fair contribution towards meeting community needs and the protection of the community's resources and legitimate interests. One of George's particular crusades was pursuing those responsible for damage done to the roads by 'snigging', a term that refers to the ruts gouged into road surfaces by logs dragged behind teams of horses or bullocks. Such a practice was commonplace in the district, as a result of the extensive logging operations over many years. It was a sensitive issue in the relations between loggers and farmers. George found this practice to be particularly antisocial, one that caused damage and was a cost to the whole community, resulting from the carelessness or selfishness of a few. One can imagine this offending the morality of the part-time preacher.

George was not only earnest in his role on the board, he also conducted himself with a good degree of ethical probity. In his last year as a representative on the board, 1900, the board minutes record that he 'retired from the table' for the discussion and decision-making in relation to a matter in which it seems he may have had a personal interest. The issue in question was the relocation of the original board hall. The matter was contentious and the votes on the board were split. It is not clear what the precise nature of any conflict of interest may have been. Nonetheless, in the interests of good governance, George appears to have taken a principled position and absented himself from the vote.

Overall, George discharged his duties on the board with a great deal of energy and conscientiousness. He was forced by ill health to step down from the board in February 1897 and it is notable that the board at its next meeting passed the following motion:

> That a vote of thanks be tendered to Mr Fewtrell for his past services and a letter written to him conveying the thanks of the Board and stating that the Board are very sorry that through his services he is suffering such bad health.

The nature of George's illness at the time is not known, although it could be thought to have been over exertion and some form of physical breakdown. It seems also that the collapse in his health was related to 'his services', suggesting that his commitment while admirable was detrimental to his welfare. The episode, however, did not stop George for long, as he was back on the board in February 1898. A month earlier he was appointed a Justice of the Peace in the colony of Queensland. Clearly he was committed to the work and effective in the role. He stepped down finally from the board at the end of 1900. Indicative of the growth in the region, the board became the Maroochy Shire Council in 1902.

11

The yeoman builds a nation

The Fewtrell household and orchards continued to grow throughout the decades of the 1880s and 1890s. George's involvement in the community and the various causes associated with building a pioneer community were ultimately secondary to the task of supporting a growing family and building a sustainable farming enterprise. Work on both fronts grew in terms of demands and scale. For Elise, the daily routines of homestead living with a young family were all the more onerous due to limitations in her movement. As the family grew and the children became older, they were able to take on larger roles in running the household. Discipline and organisation were key elements of the homestead routine. George, while gregarious and enjoying the company of others, was a rather firm taskmaster.

The house was augmented by the construction of a secondary structure that abutted it to the rear. The kitchen was in the linking space, a stair or two down from the main house. It contained a large kitchen table, a fuel stove (replacing the original open fire) and a kitchen safe for keeping food, an ongoing challenge in the climate. At the rear of the house were an outside boiler that served as a clothes washing area, and a large water tank. Sam, the youngest child, remembered his mother sewing clothes, making jam and doing most of the cooking and food preparation in the early years. Over time Maria, Annie and Emma gradually took on those roles, as Elise's movements became increasingly restricted. The family had a regular supply of meat from the nearby butcher, who received his supplies via the afternoon train.

The Fewtrell family at Homestead 4171. Elise is seated on the veranda, with George standing to her left. George's daughter from his first marriage, Maria, is on the far left with her husband and children. George's son, Henry, stands next to George. George and Elise's children stand below (L to R) Sam, young George, Anna and Emma. (From The Palmwoods Story.)

The arrival of the train flagged the need for young Sam to go off and pick up the meat order.

The household kept a few cows for milk, along with a small piggery and fowls. Within a hundred metres of the house was a range of farm equipment and resources, including the orchard barn. Sam recalled in his later years that the barn was made of beech timber, notable in that high-quality timber was put to such a utilitarian function. The reality was that they used the resources readily available to them at the time. The household had several horses, two for general transportation and another, called Nugget, was used mostly for work in the orchard.

The orchard required a routine of tasks and responsibilities in a sequence that followed the cycle of nature. Initially, oranges were the principal crop of the orchard, with mandarins being secondary in terms of quantity of production. All hands were required to help out in the orchard at key times and, while Maria and Annie preferred the household work, Emma was especially skilled at grading and packing the fruit.

The barn was the centre for such activity, with the fruit being held there after picking and then graded and boxed prior to despatch. The dray was used principally to transport the packed fruit to the nearby railway station. Young Henry and George James also worked in the orchard and as the years passed George employed a local man to help with the orchard work, and no doubt ease the burden on himself. The climate brought its own challenges. Palmwoods had an average annual rainfall of 65 inches, with 103 days being classified as wet days. Rain and humidity were most plentiful in the January to March period, causing mildew and fungus on the fruit which, combined with infestations of red scale, required regular spraying with a cyanide solution and the installation of large canvas coverings.

At some stage during these years, George sold a few acres of his property adjacent to the railway, on which land Walker's sawmill was established. This facility subsequently supplied many of the wood blocks that were used in constructing the main thoroughfares of Sydney. The streets of Sydney may not have been lined with gold, but they were built with vast numbers of beautiful rainforest timber blocks, sourced from the Palmwoods mill.

The work was constant and arduous and the rewards, while ample, were a struggle from year to year. Sam recalled that his father had one very good year where the conditions were auspicious and the crop excellent. That particular year enabled George to clear his commitments and get ahead – presumably providing a modest buffer for the inevitable hard years that would follow. The farming settlers of Queensland in general did it tough through this period. There was much experimentation with crops and soil conditions to find the most suitable crops with which to persist.

George was now a settled fruit grower, focused on citrus and creating the best conditions in the orchard for plant growth and development. Also in his mind, however, was how best to get his produce to market, the logistics and costs involved and indeed the extent and reliability of those markets. The critical elements for George were to ensure that there were keen buyers for produce and to progressively diversify the range of markets available for that produce. With those thoughts in mind, he then moved to the next level of thinking and began to realise that some potential markets could only be reached if the fruit itself was capable of being transported longer distances without damage or deterioration. So what types of citrus would travel best and for longer periods and how could he, as the grower, use his skills to develop and refine the keeping qualities of the fruit? Markets in Sydney and Melbourne were within range. Other possibilities, such as supplying produce to the London market, would mean that fruit would need to withstand a shipping journey of three or more months. This was certainly daunting, but worth considering as a developmental target.

In addition to attending to the general operations of the orchard, George had a separate corner where he experimented with root and bud stock. This process extended over several years, gradually working with plants that exhibited the desired qualities and refining their attributes so that they more consistently displayed the characteristics required. Nature works to its own rhythm and this was painstaking, tedious work. It also required a logical approach, although occasionally Nature itself could surprise and throw up its own variation – known in the industry as a 'sport'.

George had two objectives: to develop a fruit that would mature early and could be delivered to local and regional markets ahead of other varieties and one that, once picked, would hold its condition and be suitable for shipping to overseas markets. In this, he aimed to bring together his own market-savvy assessment of what he perceived to be a business opportunity with the farming and plant husbandry skills he had first observed in Shropshire. In the case of the latter, he was directly applying techniques and cultures which Charles Darwin had observed so keenly and invoked in his writing. George did this by observing and noting varieties that showed promise of the desired qualities and then experimenting with blending those attributes with other robust, well-performing citrus lines.

As the decade of the 1890s drew to a close, Elise and George at times must have reflected that they had not fared too badly since their earlier travails. For George, his year of sadness, 1881, was now well behind him. In the intervening period, he had established a frontier home and his family was growing around him. They were by now a well-integrated young adult family that supported him in his work and the income stream it generated for the family. Elise also had reason to feel satisfied and probably somewhat surprised that, despite her four years of unremitting trauma and sadness, she too had survived and was now content in her new home, surrounded by four children of her own. She had prevailed long enough to appreciate that 'other little ones come to somewhat fill the aching void'. Above all, she was safe and supported. Family, her first priority in life, was safe and nurtured.

George was demonstrating his worth as a Queensland yeoman farmer, a man who had succeeded in his new land and was his own master. Certainly he was operating on a wider canvas than he might ever have thought possible in Shropshire. His horizons were broader and his fortunes more assured. As he observed the growing debate about federation of the Australian colonies, it is unlikely he would have been among the naysayers, although many of his fellow Queenslanders were. He may have looked at the emerging labour movement and its growing political arm with a sceptical eye, but he was overall a very positive person, one who would think that the land to which he had been drawn, and in which he was now at home, would fare well in the future as a distinct federated entity, within the overall bosom of the Empire.

On the federation question, George is likely to have taken his cue from Samuel Griffith, the man who had championed the yeoman farmer ideal and lead the push for more progressive development in Queensland. Griffith was an ardent advocate of federation and a key player in writing one of the early draft constitutions for a united Australia. In the view of one expert, he was 'the most gifted jurist and constitutional scholar to engage in the federal movement, and had the greatest individual influence on the shape of the federal constitution'.

While many within Queensland were squabbling over further division of the colony of Queensland into separate entities, Griffith had his focus on a greater Queensland as a state in a federated Australia. That vision is likely to have appealed to George Fewtrell.

Since his arrival in the colony, George had been increasingly aware that the opportunity and scope that he had to create his own future were linked, in large measure, to being able to participate in the democratic decision-making of the Queensland community. The right to vote was not something that he had experienced or even expected back in England. Here, however, it was his right and an opportunity to participate in the building of his community and country. Here, his horizons were not narrowed by the hedgerows of English lanes, rather they were limited only by the imagination and the broader consensus of his fellow man. Being a Queenslander was a good way to be a solid man of the British Empire. He did not need to be naturalised when he arrived in the colony – being British meant that he was 'in' from the moment he stepped off the boat.

For Elise, it was different. She was of German nationality – by virtue of being from Holstein. But George's Britishness became her passport too as, by marrying George, Elise also became a British subject. She did not need to seek formal naturalisation, as she was now George's wife and George was British, albeit now Queensland British and soon to be Australian British. Her sister, Catherina, on the other hand, had needed to formally apply for naturalisation, which she lodged with the Queensland authorities before federation. Her marriage to the earlier naturalised Peter Kuskopf did not bring with it the same automatic change in her identity.

While Queensland may have had a difficult time of it in the 1880s and 1890s, George and Elise now lived in what was considered the wealthiest country on earth. Their futures lay here. They did not look back and hanker for things gone. Both had been shaped by their experiences of the last 25 years in this new land. Gradually they had come to view it with less of the bewilderment that they may have experienced initially. Both seemed content and at home in Palmwoods. For George, this had always been easier, with less ambiguity to interpret and fewer negotiations to feel comfortable in its patterns and rhythms.

For Elise, their place at Palmwoods was where her family was flourishing. Elise may have reflected that as an adult she had now lived longer in Palmwoods than anywhere else. She probably thought of herself as a resident of Palmwoods who previously lived in Schleswig-Holstein, now Germany. Although on paper she was British, her change of nationality was a bureaucratic construct that required little of her hand or heart. It was probably an abstract concept that in reality meant little to her. But she was a recognised woman in Palmwoods, the lady with the limp, the wife of George and the mother of a large family of growing Queenslanders, British Australians or, as some would simply say, Australians.

In the end, their hopes for federation were not disappointed. Queensland voted in favour, but by the narrowest margin of any state. Brisbane, after a bitterly fought campaign, marked by violence and civic disturbance, voted No by a staggering 60 per cent plus, the highest negative vote of any of the Australian capital cities. Parts of western Queensland also voted very strongly against federation, followed by parts of central Queensland. The north of Queensland was strongly supportive. Gympie, the strong mining town to the north of Palmwoods and stronghold of the emerging Labor Party, voted in favour of federation, due largely to the campaigning efforts of local representative and future Labor prime minister Andrew Fisher.

It was George's custom to gather the family on Sundays for a roast dinner at Homestead 4171, on the side of the hill, looking east across the valley towards Woombye. They were events of some occasion. He would wear his coat and sit at the head of the table. As was typical of the times, it was a very patriarchal household. The women, of course, had prepared the meal. These were occasions George enjoyed. Many years later, it was remembered that the

> home was open house for those who sought his companionship

and help. Many of the seasonal workers who travelled north by foot enjoyed the hospitality and the meal received at the Fewtrell home.

George was the man of the house. Had he remained in Shropshire, he might have continued to be a seasonal worker, or perhaps a senior farm labourer on a particular property, for a hopefully kind master. However, now he was the farmer in control of his own land, a role to which realistically he could not have aspired in Shropshire. He would have reflected with some pride on the progress of his community, and his role in its development would have given him great satisfaction.

The past decade had seen considerable growth and consolidation in the community. George's range of interests and the extent of his involvement in causes and developments also widened. Increasingly, George was thought of as a man who could sort through issues, someone who was clear-headed and looked to the future. He was repeatedly chosen to chair public meetings convened by the community or special interest groups. George was the man to whom the community turned. He had a reputation for being good on his feet and able to speak to the occasion. His contributions were described as clear and lucid. He was a man who could put together 'a natty speech', seemingly at short notice. He excelled in this regard in both social and industry settings. His shins remained sharp!

While his active role in the early establishment of the Palmwoods district was largely complete, it would be seen as having been something of an apprenticeship for his focus in the next decade – the development of the citrus industry and strengthening the commercial prospects of the broader region. Palmwoods was now part of a federated Australia, a nation for a continent, made up of six very competitive states. Many residents of the now state of Queensland retained a pre-eminent loyalty to their own parts of the northern state. That 'Queensland nativism' was built on a growing sense that they were a people who could develop their land through their own energies and enterprise, overcome its enervating heat and other challenges and manage their own affairs to the greatest extent possible. George would have shared this view, up to a point. His horizons were wider than most. In the work that lay ahead of him in the new century, he would come to focus on urging others to move beyond their parochialism.

He would be well placed to undertake this challenge within the citrus industry. By early in the decade, he had succeeded in developing a mandarin that could be picked early and had good keeping qualities, meaning it was capable of being exported, could retain its quality for an extended period and still be highly presentable to customers. This had included painstaking work over a number of years as he grafted bud stock of plants that offered promise of desired characteristics and commercially exploitable features. His refined mandarin would be able to reach new markets and provide the grower with more diversified and reliable income streams. It was sometimes referred to as a shipping mandarin, but in the district was known as Fewtrell's Early mandarin. This fruit was a home-grown Palmwoods product, a talisman for the local citrus industry that was fast becoming the centre of citrus growing in Queensland.

12

A man with wide horizons

In the first decade after federation, the fortunes of the fruit industry, particularly citrus, largely determined the fortunes of the towns around Nambour. Progress associations and farmers' groups were formed in most small communities, reflecting the symmetry of successful citrus farms and prosperous towns. Palmwoods growers formed a fruit growers' association in the late 1890s and the Palmwoods Progressive and Industrial Association was established shortly afterwards. George was involved in both of these initiatives. Other towns in the district took similar steps. In many instances, areas were effectively competing with each other in terms of developing civic amenities and promoting produce for market. The progress associations were the focus of the former, while the fruit growers' associations principally addressed fruit marketing.

There was great vibrancy in the communities of the district, demonstrated by industry on the farms and enthusiasm in the communities. In addition to citrus, experimentation with crops ranged across coffee, sugar, bananas and pineapples. In the early years, this sometimes included dual crops, such as pineapples growing among citrus trees, in an effort to reduce soil run-off. Inevitably, each crop encountered problems, either in the reliability or robustness of plants for the conditions, or problems in getting the fruit to market in a presentable state and at a viable price. In one sense, the area was an ideal experimental outpost for fruit production and marketing in the new state, being located reasonably close to Brisbane, with regular and direct rail services. The greater Brisbane area provided a ready and expanding market, having grown from a town of 37,000 in 1881 to around 120,000 in 1901.

The Palmwoods growers were early advocates of cooperative and district-wide approaches to the industry. They were also insightful in identifying limitations in traditional operating approaches, and both creative and energetic in proposing solutions. For example, in the mid-1890s, the Palmwoods growers introduced a cooperative buying scheme that enabled their members to participate in group buying arrangements as a way of reducing production costs. They were also focused on improving processes for getting fruit to market. In addition to packing and presentation issues, they were active in negotiating with the rail authorities for dedicated services to convey fruit to market at key times, and the provision of cool chambers to reduce product loss.

Over and above all of these issues was the need to achieve more cooperation among growers so that markets could be opened up and serviced, not by a single entrepreneurial grower for a week or two, but by a district and groups of growers who could provide a prolonged and assured source of product. This was a challenging concept for many growers, who personified the sole operator/producer ideal and greatly valued being able to do things in their own accustomed ways. A first step in implementing these changes was to build larger grower associations that spoke for and acted on behalf of groups of growers and could drive innovative practices more broadly across the industry.

The late 1890s and first decade of the 1900s was a time of increasing awareness and communication among farmer groups in various regions and industries. A major catalyst in this process was the establishment by the Queensland government of the Department of Agriculture in 1887, and in particular the establishment by that agency of the *Queensland Agricultural Journal* in 1897. These initiatives provided farmers generally, and citrus growers in particular, with scientific advice and assistance and a means of communicating and promoting ideas on plant husbandry, grower organisation and industry development. A conference that would prove to be highly significant for the prospects of the industry was held in Bundaberg in June of 1901, facilitated and supported by the department.

In late 1900, a paper was presented to the Palmwoods Progressive and Industrial Progress Association dealing with the export and packing of citrus fruits. The paper, presented by Mr H. Goddard, was notable for its vision and clarity. It proposed cooperative buying arrangements, creative marketing approaches and thoughtful ways to sell into overseas markets, particularly London. George Fewtrell, as the driving force in the Palmwoods association, was strongly behind such ideas and no doubt took much of this thinking to the Bundaberg conference, to which he was a delegate. But the delegates were not just sharing their thinking. In many instances, they had put these ideas into practice, such as the shipping of mandarins to London, packed in specially designed boxes and presented attractively to appeal to the luxury market. This was done 'by packing the fruit in small three dozen cases with an edging of lace paper and a small label bearing the name "Queensland Mandarins" with the grower's initials in the centre'.

At that conference, George's fellow delegate, Mr F.J. Johnson of Palmwoods, delivered a paper on 'The orange industry in the Maroochy district'. This paper focused on export possibilities for both oranges and mandarins. In considering the latter, Johnson commented,

> Another variety which has only recently been introduced is one called Fewtrell's Shipping Mandarin and raised by Mr Fewtrell of Palmwoods. This mandarin, when known will be found worthy of a place in any orangery. The fruit comes in very early and has been known to keep in good condition for upwards of four months. This alone will testify to its value for exportation. The first time this mandarin was shown it gained the first prize at an exhibition, where it was remarked that the mandarins were much above the ordinary standard, and it has again achieved the same success within the past few weeks.

From all accounts, the Bundaberg conference proved seminal in the development of agriculture in Queensland. Its outcomes were described at the time as 'far-reaching'. The *Queensland Agricultural Journal* was rather effusive in its analysis:

> ...the work of the Conference was entrusted to a body of thoughtful, highly intelligent, practical men – men with no small parochial ideas, men who can look ahead, and, pre-seeing either danger or prosperity in the near future, came to that Conference prepared for either lot. But they came armed with facts and figures incontrovertible and undeniable, and brought to bear on the discussions the whole weight of their long practical experience.

Certainly for the citrus industry, which was now seen as being principally based in the Maroochy area, it validated much of the thinking that was taking place at the local community level. It also confirmed that grower associations based on wider geographic areas were essential to building an industry capability, rather than an individual grower or town focus. Throughout the next decade, the composition and base of grower representation morphed and changed a number of times. George was instrumental in expanding grower representation to cover what was then termed the whole of the north coast – basically north of Brisbane to a point south of Rockhampton. This became known as the North Coast Central Association, formed in 1903 with George Fewtrell as president. The annual report of the association in December 1904 indicated that it had been very active on a range of fronts, including the need to provide telegraph and telephone services to Palmwoods. The meeting was advised that at the end of its operating year the organisation had a bank balance of £2.9s.6d. Consistent with its charter, the association's meetings were held at a range of different centres. Palmwoods, however, had assumed a critical role for the industry, being the principal loading point for citrus production for much of the surrounding area.

The town of Palmwoods was a vibrant centre during these years. It was a place that in many ways realised the optimism of federation, built on the energies and ideas of its settlers. The population almost

Gathering of North Coast fruit growers at Woombye in 1904. George, as president, is in the front row, fifth from the left.

doubled between 1893 and 1897. Crop yields in the early years of the decade were particularly good. In March 1902, Palmwoods produced 8,000 cases of citrus, much of it destined for southern outlets.

It was around this time that the first proposals were made for the construction of a Buderim to Palmwoods tramway, owned by a group of farmers who donated strips of land for the route. The tramway would facilitate transportation of produce to the railway hub at Palmwoods, for forwarding to Brisbane. This was a vision that would take another decade to realise, being opened in 1915. This narrow gauge (two foot six inch) railway would however greatly raise awareness of Palmwoods as, in addition to getting the produce to market, it attracted many travellers from Brisbane, who took delight in holidaying in the rarefied air of Buderim Mountain. The Palmwoods Hotel opened in 1913 in readiness for the influx and attracted further holidaymaker clientele. The local tramway continued to operate until 1935, a testament to the entrepreneurial spirit of the local farming community and a sign of the town's success. Ultimately, the tramway lost out to improved roads in the area.

As with his earlier civic involvements, George's commitment

was constant and long-term. He did step down as chairman of the association in 1906 but continued to be a regular attendee, something that he saw as an essential commitment if such organisations were to be successful on behalf of their members. At a meeting of the association at Woombye in June 1906, the then president noted that the members 'were very much pleased to see our pioneer North Coaster, Mr G. Fewtrell, present again after his recent serious accident, hearty as ever'. The nature of the accident is unknown, but George was at further meetings that year, including the December meeting at which his son-in-law Henry Bendixon presented a paper on 'The objects of the North Coast Association'. In speaking to the paper, George said that the intention was to show that the association had justified its existence, although he thought that it could still have done more.

> Under the old system all that the Association could do was to consult with others…by bringing them into touch with their neighbours, the Association had accomplished something that justified its existence.

Clearly, George was offering the benefit of his experience and his wisdom as guidance, but there is also the suggestion that he was now beginning to think of his legacy. He seems also to have displayed a perhaps understandable sense of ownership, if not for the organisation itself, then for the vision that prompted it. He continued to make a constructive contribution in the years ahead, serving on the committee for some years and chairing meetings when requested, which occurred regularly. In this latter period, the citrus growers of the area experimented with forming subsidiary companies to implement their distribution and marketing initiatives. These operated in the main market centres, receiving fruit from growers and then arranging shipping and agency concessions.

This reinforced the innovative reputation that the area had acquired in earlier times and added to the legacy about which George seemed to ponder. His instincts were right. The ideas and actions of the early fruit growers from the Maroochy area would come to be seen as the start of a unique Queensland approach to fruit marketing. More than 60 years later, a review of the history of the development of fruit marketing in Queensland concluded that the thinking and initiatives of the early growers from the Palmwoods and Maroochy area were highly significant in the overall direction and success of fruit marketing in the state. That system was based on active grower engagement and a form of cooperation that optimised the collective strength of the growers in both fruit production and marketing. This created a platform that, in time, was supported and facilitated by government prescription.

13

Growing and going in all directions

Over the years, Elise and Catherina corresponded with siblings and their families back in Kellinghusen and the surrounding district. The correspondence was regular but not intense, sufficient to keep the two sisters up to date with news from home and the progress of their nieces and nephews. Sam recalled in his later days how both Elise and Catherina (known affectionately in the Fewtrell household as Aunty Kuskopf), would chatter away in their native tongue – a German lowlands dialect – discussing news from Kellinghusen. Fragments of only two letters survive, one sent to Elise in February 1889 by their brother Gustav and another in November 1910 addressed to Catherina from the husband of their sister Bertha. Both contain chatty information of family members, but in Gustav's letter there is reference to certain documentation that he is asking Elise to complete and return. The matter is unclear, but in part he urges her to enlist the support of the consul in order to gather certain information necessary for a submission to the authorities.

In both places, the families were expanding and weddings became a regular topic in letters and conversation. Life was moving in both the northern and southern hemispheres. The next generation was emerging, finding work which often involved leaving home, and setting up their own households. In Palmwoods, they were emerging as young Queenslanders and Australians, older than their even younger country. In Kellinghusen, they were Holstein-born Germans, some of whom, along with friends, had joined or had partners who were members of the German army, belonging to regiments garrisoned in the nearby centres of Flensburg and Keel.

Elise's declining health meant that she was less able to move outside of the family home. By around 1907, she was effectively bedridden from the damage done years earlier in that storm that ravaged the vessel on her journey south and had tormented her life ever since. Thirty years had now passed but the legacy of multiple pregnancies and births, combined with the exertions involved in frontier housekeeping and the care of children, had gradually taken their toll on her body. Sam recalled that Maria assumed the main role of running the house. He remembered her as being an assertive and organised person who would 'take charge' and 'get on with things'. Maria made sure that Sam, despite being the youngest, was an active contributor, although in his mind he ended up doing 'all the things the others didn't want to do'.

George and Elise as an older couple. (From The Nambour Chronicle, 5 October 1972.)

With her world now limited to virtually the four walls of her bedroom, Elise felt increasingly isolated from much of the bubbling activity of the homestead. The chatter and activity in the house would have made her recall, perhaps with increasing fondness, the busy childhood home that she had experienced. To lessen her sense of withdrawal, the family organised for a mirror to be placed strategically on an inner wall, facing the window. This gave Elise a perspective of the world outside from her bed. She could see down the hill to the railway station and was able to keep watch for visitors approaching the homestead. In this way, she was connected visually to the town and its increasingly busy railway hub.

Palmwoods had become the acknowledged centre of the citrus industry in Queensland, along with Woombye and other neighbouring settlements on the range to the west. Within this broader community, the Fewtrell family was itself expanding. Maria married Henry Bendixen, son of fellow Schleswig-Holstein pioneers, and Emma married into the Stanton family. Annie married Donald Mowat, a carpenter who became the first builder in Palmwoods. Both Henry and Donald became solid companions of George. Henry worked in the fruit growing industry and was supportive of George in his progress association activities. George had a high opinion of Donald, as he arranged for him to be added as an executor to his will. George had made his will in 1898, when aged 54 and at the height of his involvement in civic and citrus affairs. He nominated his executors as Elise, Henry Bendixon, and his two older sons, Henry and George James. However, in 1906 he signed a codicil, adding Donald Mowat to the list. It seems clear that he valued Donald's judgement and business acumen.

George maintained his wide interests in what could be considered an active retirement. His interest and commitment to the citrus industry was undimmed. He was now the distinguished elder in the community – an active community man and also still a firm Empire man. He now shared a name with his sovereign and in May of 1911 he was acknowledged as a donor to the King George Coronation Presentation Fund. King George, like George himself, had undertaken the sea voyage to Australia in 1880. He returned in 1901, as the Duke of Cornwall and York, to officiate at the opening of the first federal parliament in Melbourne in May 1901. The new nation may have federated under the name of Australia, but it was pre-eminently a loyal part of the Empire, whose people were British.

George's eldest son Henry, seemingly was not attracted to a career in the orchard or citrus business and at an early age headed for Sydney, choosing to deploy his entrepreneurial talents in a range of city-based business endeavours. Young George worked in the orchard for several years, but there were fewer opportunities for his younger brother Sam, who also elected to try his luck in Sydney in his early 20s. These two young men seemingly were destined to go in different directions from an early age. The experiences of each would help to shape their own identities. In a general sense, however, young George would appear to have been closer to his father, while Sam, whether by virtue of being the youngest or simply as a result of the lottery of genetics, seemed more attuned to his mother, sensitive to her frailties and feelings.

Sam recalled that he often spoke with his mother about Schleswig-Holstein. She would tell him of the uncertainty and fear that they lived with, of 'hearing shooting' and of soldiers moving through the district. Always, it seemed, they were wondering what was going to happen next. He spoke of Elise as having 'a gentle nature' – a description that his own children and grandchildren would later apply to him. It is not surprising that, as the youngest of her children, Sam would have spent more time with his mother than perhaps any of his siblings. In earlier years, there would have been too much busyness in the house, too many chores to be done. It is possible Elise saw in Sam not just the youngest of her children, but perhaps a young man who carried her thoughts back to those first three babies she bore to Carl, whose lives were snuffed out before they could really begin. Sam, by being her last child, had closed the circle on a life that straddled trauma, continents and identities. He also bore the memory of her father in his second name. She was grateful that now both she and her children could live their lives in peace.

Elise was known within the family and by others in the Palmwoods community as a quiet, shy woman, with a rolling limp. However, perhaps Elise also had a mischievous element to her character. During the later years of her life, from around the time she became bedridden, Elise had the habit each evening of having a glass of alcohol and toasting the Kaiser. This became something of her signature. It certainly prompted puzzling chuckles among the rest of her family.

The time would come, however, when such a seemingly light-hearted gesture could be seen as layered with intrigue.

In October 1912, the progress of Palmwoods received a major fillip with the auction of

> the famous big paddock – on [the] main Palmwoods–Montville Road – right at the rising town of Palmwoods – 600 acres – finest pineapple, citrus fruit, and agricultural land in the district – subdivided into 24 farms, 10 to 40 acres each.

The auction was an all-round success. In total, 18 of the blocks were sold for an overall sale price of £3,351.18.3. The vendor considered the prices fair and the buyers, reported to be 'mostly genuine settlers', were satisfied that they 'got good land at bargain prices'. George would have been pleased that his old mantra 'that the land be thrown open for selection' was still being applied and that the town was attracting keen interest. Palmwoods was indeed a town on the move.

For George, however, his declining physical health meant that he gradually withdrew from active work in the orchard. While he retained a keen interest in the fortunes of the industry and would regularly attend meetings of local growers, he began to contemplate the best arrangements for the future and finally sold the orchard and homestead as a going concern to the Briggs family in 1913. This must have been a difficult decision given that the property, its house and productive acres had been almost wholly his creation. Nevertheless, the declining health of both Elise and himself required practical decisions to be taken. Following the sale, George and Elise moved to live with their daughter Annie and husband Donald, who resided elsewhere in Palmwoods.

While George was in the process of withdrawing from the physical side of citrus growing, he nonetheless continued to have an influential role in industry forums and policy-making. In August 1912, he was elected a vice president of the Palmwoods Central Progress Association. Several days later, he was also elected to the same role with the local branch of the Queensland Farmers Union (QFU). At the time, there was much discussion that the progress association should 'unite with the local branch of the QFU'. However, this was defeated, on the basis that such a merger would be contrary to the rules of the association. Along with one other Palmwoods veteran, Mr C. Cotterell, George emerged as executive members of both organisations, no doubt with the expectation that they would ensure close liaison between both.

George's involvement with the QFU gave him entrée into the world of political policy-making for agricultural industries. In August 1913, George chaired a meeting of the Palmwoods branch of the QFU, principally devoted to examining the whole of 'the platform policy of the Country Liberal Party'. The report of the meeting in the *Nambour Chronicle* records that the matter was to remain confidential at that time, but that a few amendments were suggested. This was a time of growing political instability. Around this time, there was increasing concern in conservative ranks, both in Queensland and nationally, at the potential for the trade union movement to deliver government to the ALP, a scenario that was to play out at each level in 1914 and 1915 respectively. Although Queensland had gone to the polls in April of 1912 and elected a conservative government, it was to be the last for some time, as the ALP won government in its own right for the first time at the subsequent election. At a federal level, conservative leader Joseph Cook had defeated the ALP government of Andrew Fisher in May of 1913, but would go on to lose a double dissolution election to Fisher 18 months later, in September 1914.

It seems likely that this policy consultative process was taking place against the background of the conservative parties seeking to shore up their support in farming areas, in the face of increasing agricultural worker militancy. Whatever may have been the background, George was now in a position of having some influence on matters relating to broader industry policy. He would have enjoyed such a role and would have brought his considerable experience to the task. Given his background and the values that informed his yeoman farmer life, it seems likely that George was very comfortable within the policy framework of the conservative side of politics. He was a thoroughly decent, conservative man with a substantial record of commitment and achievement in building the sort of agrarian communities to which he was originally attracted and recruited.

14

A declaration and a death

The year of 1913 was one of foreboding. Around the world all eyes were focused on Europe and the grinding, seemingly irresistible drift to conflict between the major powers. The leaders of Germany, France, Britain and Russia were each rehearsing scenarios that might, or might need to, unfold if events got out of hand. Almost unexpectedly in June 1888, following the premature death of his father, Frederick III, Germany's young Kaiser Wilhelm II had become emperor at age 29. The reign of Frederick had lasted a mere three months after he had become Kaiser on the death of the long-lived Wilhelm I.

While crown prince, young Wilhelm had often clashed with Chancellor Bismark and the two were destined to have a brief and acrimonious relationship once Wilhelm became emperor. His break with Bismarck, 18 months after becoming emperor, removed the one strong restraining influence on Wilhelm. Bismarck had serious misgivings about Wilhelm II, eldest grandson of Queen Victoria:

> The Kaiser is like a balloon. If you do not hold fast to the string, you never know where he will be off to.

With Bismarck no longer there to 'hold fast to the string', Wilhelm proceeded down a path that engaged the militarists, gradually placed himself in total control of foreign and defence policy and set in train events that ensured a nationalist and imperialist drift into war.

While war was on many minds, it was least expected that it would be sparked by the assassination in Sarajevo of the heir apparent to the Hapsburg empire, Archduke Franz Ferdinand, who had visited Australia in 1893. In any case, by mid-1914, Australia was focused on its own political struggles at the federal level and the novelty of the nation having to go to the polls in successive years for its first double dissolution election. Within weeks of the Sarajevo shooting, the Australian Governor-General, Sir Rohan Munro Ferguson, received a cable from London advising that Australia should adopt a 'precautionary phase' for war. This was in accordance with established imperial defence arrangements, as it was not until 1942 that Australia would assert an independent foreign affairs policy stance.

In response to the cable advice, similar statements of support were made by the incumbent prime minister Joseph Cook and his alternative Andrew Fisher (at separate election campaign meetings), indicating Australia was up for the fight. The parliament had already been dissolved, but the federal cabinet met promptly and offered to place the Australian fleet under Admiralty control and to send an expeditionary force to assist. The expiry in early August of Britain's ultimatum to Germany regarding Belgium meant that the British Empire was automatically at war, and so therefore was Australia. The Australian Constitution was (is) silent on the matter of a declaration of war and the prevailing view was that 'the creation of a state of war and the establishment of peace necessarily resided in the Sovereign himself as the Head of the Empire'.

Adding to the confusion and lack of clarity around the identity of the state as an institution with authority to announce and prosecute a war, the Governor-General chose to forward to all state governors the cable he had received from London that stated, 'War has broken out with Germany. Send all State Governors.' When this was received by the Queensland governor, he duly informed the premier of Queensland. The premier subsequently 'took the extraordinary measure of issuing his own proclamations' in the name of Queensland as a sovereign state. This was followed up by another remarkable piece of statecraft, when the Queensland lieutenant-governor, who was also president of the Legislative Council and vice-admiral of the state of Queensland, issued an independent proclamation that war had broken out between His Majesty and the German emperor and that all enemy shipping would be confiscated under the terms of imperial legislation. Other declarations would soon be made that would highlight further the sometimes elusive nature of identity, formal and informal, and require it to be sworn before the courts.

While Australia's national government seemed not to be empowered technically and culturally to declare war, it was a curious fact that the government of one of its constituent states, Queensland, saw itself as sufficiently emboldened and legally empowered to issue its own declaration of war. The Australian state, like many of its residents, was grappling with its new identity, struggling to understand what it could do and what it should do, and to make choices between the two. The states may have federated under the banner of the Commonwealth of Australia, but the view prevailed that the states persisted as entities in their own right under British law and custom. Australian identity was a mere subset of the generic and a more fundamental British identity. Well into its second decade as a federated nation, the Australian state was still entangled in the old vines of colonialism, highlighting that culturally the country's outlook had not changed dramatically and that the words of the Constitution Act were still to come to life in the forums and hearts of the nation.

While the nation's politicians were thinking about war and busy canvassing votes, George put considerable energy into the establishment of a branch of the Patriotic Fund in Palmwoods, in support of the war effort and care for the wounded and the families of those who might be killed. In late July 1914, he was called on to chair a meeting of the Palmwoods community to consider a proposal for a tramway between Palmwoods and Montville. Recruitment for the war began enthusiastically in Palmwoods, as it did in other centres around the country. The federal election proceeded on Saturday 5 September in what gave all the indications of being a tight contest. It was some days before the tallies were sufficiently advanced to reveal that Labor's Andrew Fisher would once again form a government, the priorities of which would be focused overwhelmingly on winning the war.

In the midst of all these happenings, George was struck down with a stroke on Monday 7 September 1914 and died the following day. His doctor certified that he lingered only for 16 hours. George's death was a great shock to Elise and the family. It was also a shock and a severe blow to the Palmwoods community. In his very active life, George may have been susceptible to stress and overexertion. He had been forced to rest from overwork while a member of the divisional board and, from all accounts, he seemed to have been a man who never stopped working on something. Much of the pressure in his life was probably the result of his own driving passion to do things, to get things done, to make a contribution and grow the community and his family.

It had been a little more than 40 years since he disembarked the *Winefred* on 14 January 1874. In that time, he had contributed manfully to the development of the colony, now state, of Queensland. He had fulfilled his commitment to bring to the fields of Queensland the vision of the yeoman farmer. His contribution had gone far beyond what might have been expected of him, in both agricultural and civic terms. He had produced and raised two families, recovering from a low point in 1881 to gather around him another family that had now gone forth as young Queenslanders and Australians. His second wife had been his unlikely companion for more than 30 years, a quiet woman whose inner strength he could but admire and indeed love. Elise was once again a widow. Now George was gone, probably without the chance to really say goodbye. This time, however, she would be surrounded by her own flesh and blood, who would hold her firm in this latest storm.

On Friday 11 September 1914, the *Brisbane Courier* printed the following obituary for George Fewtrell:

> One of the oldest pioneers of the district Mr George Fewtrell, passed away at Palmwoods on Tuesday, aged 72 years.

The late Mr Fewtrell was born at Staffordshire [sic], England, in 1842, and emigrated to Queensland 40 years ago. He resided in Toowoomba for a time, and then returned to Brisbane, where he lived until 1883. During that time he took an active part in the formation of the Ark of Safety Lodge, P.A.F.S.O.A, of which lodge, at the time of his death, he was the only surviving foundation member.

He came to Palmwoods 31 years ago, and selected land adjoining what is now the township of Palmwoods, where he lived until a year or so ago, when he disposed of the property and had been living privately since.

During his residency in Palmwoods he took an active part in every movement for the advancement of the district. He was a member of the Maroochy Shire Council for a number of years, and filled the chair during two terms. He was also on the first committee team of the local school, and was also an enthusiastic member of the Farmers' Union.

A few days before his death he was instrumental in the establishment of a Patriotic Fund at Palmwoods. His purse was always open to any deserving cause, and he was looked upon as 'the father of Palmwoods'.

He leaves a widow (who has been an Invalid for a considerable time), three sons (Messrs George, of Nambour, Samuel, and James (this refers to Henry), who reside in Sydney), and three daughters – Mesdames Mowat (Palmwoods), Bendixon (Nambour), and Stanton (Kingaroy).

The funeral took place on Wednesday, and was the largest seen in the district – the school children marched in front of the hearse to the graveside, and Mr T. Lowe (Chairman of the Maroochy Shire) represented the Council, was largely attended [sic].

George's funeral was rather hastily organised for the following day, 9 September. He was buried high on the hill of the Woombye cemetery, one of the early graves to be opened in that particular burial place, established to service all surrounding towns. The development of the cemetery had been an early initiative of the council on which he served.

Had George not journeyed to Queensland and made the contribution he did, he would no doubt have been buried in the grounds of a local parish church in Shropshire. In Queensland, however, his world had been wider, consistent with his vision of broader horizons. His resting place is on a hill and belongs to the wider community, not one small parish. Now more than ever, he was a man of the Australian soil.

As with other communities with significant numbers of German emigrants, there was anxiety in Palmwoods that the commencement of hostilities could herald draconian provisions against non-naturalised settlers and even naturalised settlers. As the rhetoric of war and the campaign for army recruitment got under way, German-born residents began to feel increasingly vulnerable. This was understandable in the context of the growing portrayal of Germans as 'bestial huns' and other epithets. Already in August a proclamation by the governor-general had called for all subjects of the German empire resident in Australia to report to the nearest police station. On 11 August the Commissioner of Queensland Police issued an instruction to his force to 'take the necessary action in your district for fulfilment' of the governor-general's proclamation. For some time, there was confusion as to the extent that such orders placed an obligation on 'naturalised' Germans to report regularly to police. Eventually a clarification was necessary to dispense 'naturalised' Germans from the requirement.

In Elise's case, she had never been naturalised in any formalised sense, but had simply become British by virtue of marrying George. Therefore, her position could be seen as unclear, as the only relevant document was her certificate of marriage. The potential uncertainty was compounded by a proclamation from the Supreme Court of Queensland, published in the Queensland *Government Gazette* of 31 October 1914, regarding the handling of 'Probates and Letters of Administration during the continuance of the War now existing between Great Britain and Germany and Austria-Hungary'. In part, the statement advised that

> ...the grant [of probate] shall be made upon the condition that no

portion of the assets shall be distributed or paid during the war to any beneficiary or creditor who is a German or Austro-Hungarian subject wherever resident, or to anyone on his behalf, or to or on behalf of any person resident in Germany or Austria-Hungary, of whatever nationality, without the express sanction of the Crown, acting through the Attorney General…

It went on to require

Any applicant for probate or letters of administration during the war shall give such information as the Registrar may require in order to ascertain whether any of the assets would in time of peace be distributable or payable to any such subjects, and if required shall make a statutory declaration as to the assets and their disposition in the event of probate or letters of administration being granted.

Elise had no statutory documentation regarding her change of nationality, except the perhaps oblique reassurance of the record of her marriage to George. As the sole beneficiary of George's estate, she would be dependent upon the processes and practicalities of the law.

15

Son of the father, son of the mother

It is inevitable that the growing mood and fear of war would have prompted discussion in the family about enlisting for the fight. All of George's sons and his sons-in-law were of an eligible age to enlist. Given George's commitment to Empire, it would have been surprising if he had not had a conversation with George junior on the matter. One imagines that the older George would have seen it in terms of 'duty' and 'honour' to respond to the sovereign's call to defend the Empire. Exactly what Elise may have thought on the topic is unclear, but one could reasonably expect that she would have been quite torn on the matter. She had her own experience of the horrors of war, she had already lost three sons to tragedy and she would have been acutely aware that going off 'to fight the Kaiser', in practice meant going off to fight her own people, perhaps even members of her own extended family.

It is unknown what may have been in the minds of young George and Sam at the time war was declared. Among other things, George would have been looking forward to the start of the next cricket season and continuing his good form opening the batting for the Palmwoods eleven. In any case, thoughts of enlisting were overtaken swiftly by the impact of his father's death. His younger brother, Sam, had been in Sydney for some years, pursuing his own life and working on the NSW tramways. In practical terms, his life was quite separate from the day-to-day happenings in Palmwoods. He had returned to Palmwoods a year or so earlier to recuperate after being 'dusted' while working in the tram sheds of Sydney. The doctor had ordered a change of air to clear his lungs, so he took the train to Brisbane and on to Palmwoods for several weeks' rest. His arrival, unannounced, prompted great excitement when first glimpsed in the mirror by Elise, as he walked the hill leading from the station. That visit, a year or two before the outbreak of the war, was to be Sam's last meeting with his father.

Of the five executors to George's will, young George was probably the least skilled in terms of understanding its obligations and negotiating its path to probate. Elise was in no position to take a lead role, nor was Henry who was also based in Sydney. It fell to the two sons-in-law to initiate the legal processes though a firm of Nambour solicitors. The will itself was straight forward, giving to Elise all of his estate. The complication was how to respond to the edict that no German or Austrian-Hungarian national could be a beneficiary of a will. Resolution of this matter required two sworn statements by the executors, excluding Elise, effectively stating that no beneficiary to the will was 'a German or Austro-Hungarian subject'.

The matter seems also to have been complicated by Henry's absence in Sydney. A first sworn statement, signed by the four executors (minus Elise) used the formulation

> The testator was a natural born British subject, as are we these deponents, and no beneficiary under the said will nor creditor of the said testator is a German or Austro-Hungarian subject or other alien enemy of the British Crown.

This statement, although signed by the four executors in late November and early December, was insufficient to satisfy the court and another sworn statement was required. This second statement, although signed by only three of the executors (Henry being the missing signatory), seemed to be more acceptable to the court. The formulation, in relation to the matter of the nationality of a beneficiary, used in this document was more expansive:

> No portion of the assets of the said George Fewtrell deceased is

distributable or payable under his said will and codicil to any beneficiary or creditor who is a German or Austro-Hungarian subject or other alien enemy of the British Crown, wherever resident or to anyone in his lien or their behalf or to or on behalf of any persons resident in Germany or Austria Hungary or other country of whatever nationality.

The case came before the chief justice of the Supreme Court of Queensland, who granted probate on 12 January 1915. That it was considered by the chief justice and one of the first to come before the court in compliance with the proclamation, probably reflects a degree of sensitivity, to ensure that the procedures and formulations used were in order in all respects. The revised wording has a style that suggests it was seen as a template for future cases. Whatever the legal nuances in the document and the formal order of the court, it seems inevitable that Elise would have been relieved that the matter was resolved. That evening she had added reason to celebrate while proposing her customary toast: 'To the Kaiser'.

Elise's respect and admiration for the Kaiser had long been a source of puzzled mirth, a sort of discomforting fascination. The persistence of this 'gentle woman' in raising a glass to the Kaiser, even during the war years, suggests that her feelings were deeply held. But what were they and what lay behind them? It is possible that in toasting the Kaiser, Elise may have been referring either to the office of the German emperor or to the particular occupant of the time, Wilhelm II, who assumed the mantle in 1888 and held that position until forced into exile at the end of the Great War. It is possible of course that to Elise both entities of the office coexisted in her mind.

As a resident of the duchy of Holstein, one half of the province of Schleswig-Holstein, Elise would have been disposed to a link with the Prussian state, just as residents of Schleswig were historically disposed to union with the Danish state. That was the conundrum of the 'Schleswig-Holstein problem'. Both wanted to stay together, but each separately was pulled in a different direction. This dichotomy lay at the heart of the conflict that afflicted the area for a hundred years. For the Holsteiner, peace was only achieved when the Prussian state despatched the Danes and annexed the province. Only then did the hostilities cease, enabling people to go about their lives in peace. So in that sense it was the Kaiser, in the person of Wilhelm I, who had brought peace to the people of Schleswig-Holstein. Elise seems to have long carried the trauma of the hostilities, a factor that played some part in her original decision to emigrate.

Elise had left Kellinghusen for Brisbane several years before Wilhelm II became emperor. However, he would have been known to her as the young prince, grandson to Wilhelm I and son of the next in line to the throne, Frederick III. As a young man, Wilhelm II had married Augusta Victoria, known as Dona, the eldest daughter of Frederick, the Duke of Schleswig-Holstein, a statement of statecraft as much as personal affection that would not have gone unnoticed in the challenged province.

Before becoming Kaiser, the young Wilhelm had clashed with Bismarck over the chancellor's anti-worker legislation, indicating his disapproval of its draconian restrictions. On becoming Kaiser, the issue became a critical factor in the young emperor's decision to dismiss Bismarck in 1890, which not only marked the end of Bismarck's anti-socialist crusade but also the loss of a steadying chancellor's hand on the unpredictable emperor. The Bismarck–Wilhelm fall-out occurred well after Elise had arrived in Queensland. However, such developments would no doubt have been newsworthy content in letters from siblings in Kellinghusen. Given the degree of industrial unrest that prevailed in Kellinghusen in the years before Elise's departure, it would not have been surprising if Wilhelm II was considered a hero in that part of the province, and perhaps to an expatriate in Queensland. Maybe a hero worthy of a toast, particularly so if indeed her Carl had been caught up in the industrial turmoil, which could in part have prompted the decision to emigrate.

Elise's practice of still toasting the Kaiser many years after these events speaks of her ongoing affection for her homeland and perhaps also a mischievous streak in her character. She probably realised that the toast caused a degree of anxiety and dismay, but she continued with the practice as a way of making a statement about her heritage. That heritage would soon be put to the test when young George signed up to go and fight the Kaiser in Europe. As a mother, this must have been a source of great pain. War had returned to afflict her life and those she loved most dearly. It might also have seemed remarkable to her that she was officially British and would be considered an alien by her own people, just as they were by the government of the land she now called home. The world, it seemed, had changed around her.

When she and Carl, all those years ago, considered the possibility of emigrating to the colony of Queensland, a land on the other side of the earth and thousands of miles away, the thought that a child of hers might one day return to Europe as an armed combatant to fight against her own people would have seemed incomprehensible. Now its reality was closing in upon her as an elderly frail woman. War was a madness she had come to the other end of the earth to escape. No longer.

Young George signed his enlistment papers on 24 July 1915. He joined the 15th Battalion, stating that he was a sawmill hand and nominating Elise as his next of kin. He took the oath, no doubt conscious that his father would have approved.

> I George James Fewtrell swear that I will well and truly serve our Sovereign Lord the King in the Australian Imperial Force from 24 July 1915 until the end of the War, and a further period of four months thereafter unless sooner lawfully discharged, dismissed or removed there from; and that I will resist His Majesty's enemies and cause His Majesty's peace to be kept and maintained; and that I will in all matters appertaining to my service, faithfully discharge my duty according to law. So Help Me, God.

George James Fewtrell, like his father, was a man of the Empire.

George sailed for Egypt in October 1915, embarking on the troop ship *Seang Bee*, which had been built in Belfast in 1891 and remarkably had been known for the first 20 years of its commercial service as *Shropshire*. Just as his father had sailed on a ship named with Shropshire connections, so too did young George. If he had been aware, George might have seen the provenance of his own ship as a good omen for his foreign adventure. He would have been correct in doing so as, although George had a difficult war, he did survive.

George was deployed to France in June 1916 and saw action in places whose names speak of the hell with which they were associated: Armentiers, Poziers, the Somme until Bullecourt, Messines and Passchendaele. He was gassed twice. In February 1917, Elise was advised that George 'is reported wounded and remaining on duty', a message that offered its own perverse reassurance of his condition. The news could have been far worse. A later advice informed Elise that in late August 1918 George had suffered another wound. This time it was a shrapnel wound to his arm and hand that required treatment in a field hospital. That advice, however, did not reveal an even more perilous difficulty that George had experienced a month or so earlier, when he was charged with desertion and faced a court martial.

George's statement to those proceedings, defending the circumstances of his absence from his post, reveals something of the travails that the regular soldier faced in the theatre of war. The charge was of desertion from 3 July to 19 July 1918. He stated that since his arrival in France in June 1916,

> I don't think that I have had a fair deal from my Platoon officer. I appealed to him to give me a spell sometime out of the line, as I thought with my service I was entitled to it. He did not give me one and told me he needed some of the old hands. It is now – 12 months since I had leave.

His defence, virtually throwing himself on the mercy of the presiding officers, as a soldier who had done his best in difficult circumstances and tried to act honourably, won some respect from those hearing the case. He was found not guilty of desertion but guilty of absence without leave and sentenced to 30 days' internment in a field prison.

It was not long after returning to his regiment that George was again gassed and then wounded for the second time. After treatment in a field hospital for some weeks, he returned to the front line on 12 October. His war ended on the day of the armistice, 11 November 1918. Shortly afterwards he was granted leave and in early December travelled to London, where he remained on duty until cleared to return to Australia. George had endured a harrowing, but not unusual, ordeal as a servant of the King in his Australian military force. He had no doubt passed through his own passage of identity, having to deal with much that one would hope never to endure. But he had survived. His father would have been proud of him. He would have much to tell his mother on his return.

Throughout this time, his younger brother Sam, who chose not to enlist, had made his own way in Sydney working on the railways, to which service he had been transferred following his earlier ailment. He had also met a young woman, with whom he had become closely associated. Florence Conroy was descended from an Irish convict and Catholic family. Sam was a protestant. Their courtship in mid-1916 led them into a sectarian minefield of mistrust and rejection, but their feelings for each other meant that they pushed such complications aside. When Florence became pregnant in late 1916, their lives suddenly collided with the harsh sectarian world that prevailed at

Sam Fewtrell as a young man in his early 20s.

the time. Florence was disowned by her family for having brought shame to their name. She was thrown out of the family home, never to have contact again.

Florence was dependent upon the generous nature of a work colleague who took her in and gave her protection and support. Sam promised her that he would do the honourable thing and marry her. But first he needed to gather himself and chose to visit his mother and the family in Palmwoods. While on this visit, he was put under some pressure to 'forget about' this young woman in Sydney, pregnant and Catholic. He could simply stay in Queensland and start another chapter in his life. Sam, who wanted thinking time, no doubt contemplated their counsel. But he had written to Florence and given his word that she would be his wife and the child she was carrying would be theirs. He held to that position and returned to Sydney. On 15 May 1917, he and Florence were married in a brief ceremony in the sacristy of St Patrick's church, Church Hill, in central Sydney. The venue of the wedding was prescribed by the religious prejudices of the day. Sam was willing to have a Catholic wedding but Florence's church would offer only a begrudging second-class recognition of their commitment. They became parents to a son, Colin Samuel, on 10 July 1917.

Each son, George and Samuel, had followed their hearts and their consciences. George, formed in his father's image, chose to go to war in the name of his and his father's sovereign, knowing that he would be fighting his mother's people. Samuel, sensitive to his mother's heritage and feelings, turned away from the path of war, perhaps recognising the pain it would bring to his mother. He was more sensitive to his mother's story, more aware of her pain, both now and from her earlier experience of war in the lowlands of Schleswig-Holstein. The story of the two sons was in some ways a microcosm of the story of the country, as it wrestled with the question of conscription and ultimately voted against it in two referenda held during the course of the war.

Notwithstanding the cleft between the courses adopted by the two brothers, they each faced their own searching examination of their true worth as individuals and men of honour. George fought for the Empire and for himself and negotiated his survival as a sane individual in the face of the bullets and the technical rules of war. Sam faced a different moral dilemma, but one no less challenging in terms of discovering the fibre of his own identity and the values for which he stood. He kept his word to Florence. He resisted the invitation to take the easy way out and he stood firm against the sectarian temper of the times. Drawing on the exemplars of their shared but separate parents, each learned much about their real identity.

16

Endings without meetings

Palmwoods celebrated the end of the war in similar fashion to towns across the country. The great relief that the killing was over and that sons and husbands could return was news that thrilled all, Elise included. Throughout the war, Elise had lived with her eldest daughter Annie and husband Donald Mowat, a short distance out of town on the road to Montville. Donald was a carpenter, now established as the preferred house builder in Palmwoods. Elise looked forward to young George's homecoming; to being able to give her first surviving son a hug, to look at his wounds and to hear something of his experience. Not the whole details, but enough to appreciate what her son, by now a man of 30 years, had endured and overcome. He couldn't come home soon enough and, although he was now safe in London, each day that he was delayed was a day she could not see him.

She had not heard from her youngest son for some time, since his return to Sydney and marriage to Florence. She had heard that the baby was a boy but other details were scant. Sam had seemingly decided that it was probably best not to bother them with too much information about his little family in Sydney. They were on their own, making their own way through the waters of religious bigotry. But she did often wonder about him and his young son, her grandchild. His life had just begun, but hers was ebbing away.

George was finally cleared to leave England and return to Australia. He would be embarking early in April 1919. However, Elise was destined not to see either of her sons again. She died on 25 March

1919. The same doctor attended her death as had witnessed George's demise five years earlier. This time, Dr Malaher certified the cause of death as heart failure and general rheumatic debility that had left her bedridden for the past 12 years. The notice in the *Nambour Chronicle* of 4 April said simply,

> At Palmwoods, on March 25th, Engel Elise Fewtrell,
> widow of late G. Fewtrell.
> Peace and rest after a storm

Elise's funeral was held on the day following her death. She was buried next to George, high on the hill at Woombye cemetery. The reference to 'a storm' in her death notice drew attention to how fundamental an event in her life had been the shipboard incident in 1877. It marked a low point in her young life to that time and a point of affliction that would continue throughout her life. Despite all her travails, she would survive through her own inner resilience and strength. Her life would be both typical and yet instructive in understanding the journey from one identity in a northern land to another in the south. For Elise, identity had always changed around her. It had done so in Schleswig-Holstein and it did in Queensland, when she became British at the stroke of someone else's pen.

In her heart, she was probably always a young woman from Kellinghusen for whom life, in the form of war, men and circumstances, played a major role in shaping her destiny. From the time she was a young girl, she longed for peace, but would endure many storms before finally grasping it. The world was sometimes a fierce place. In her lived experience, identity was probably something of the inner life. It was more important who the person was inside. It was about that inner knowledge and confidence that could guide and sustain. In Elise's case, her identity was fused by circumstances. For some of the time, it was simply about her will to live. Not just in surviving physical and psychological traumas, but also in accepting the risk of encounter with others, that was intrinsic to recreating her life when all seemed lost. As has been said by one seer, '...the commitment to life can only come about through letting go of the need to control and accepting the risk of encounter'. Elise did that and did so at her most vulnerable. Although in one sense she had little choice open to her, in accepting the risk of the encounter with George, she won a rich prize. That prize was simply a second chance at an ordinary life. In another sense, however, it was a gift that enabled her to live again and have the family that she must have wanted desperately to be hers. Her formal identity was as a British woman, living in peace in the Australian bush, surrounded by loving and supportive family. She had joined her culture and heritage with those of George, the farmer from Shropshire, to build a local Australian community of shared genes, aspirations and values.

On his arrival back in Australia, George was discharged from the army on 14 July 1919. He was now 31 and returned to the Palmwoods district to resume his innings at the top of the order for the Palmwoods eleven. A month later, on 30 August 1919, Catherina Kuskopf (Aunty Kuskopf) died, aged 73. She had accompanied Elise on the fateful journey south, perhaps out of a sense of family concern and care for her younger sister. Her role in Elise's story was to prove pivotal in being the instrument for bringing George and Elise together. She had fulfilled her role, mothered a large family and carved out a fulfilling life for herself. She too could now take her leave.

The two brothers, George and Sam, were destined never to meet again. George married and had a family in the Nambour district. His life post-war was not easy. In a poignant echo of his father's experience, his wife died relatively young, leaving him with six children. George James did remarry but his children remained in care for several years. Sam, with Florence, raised a family of five children in Sydney and grew from being a rather stern father to a much-loved grandfather of many. In 1968, he travelled north with eldest son Colin for what would be the first meeting with his brother since before the Great War. But it was a meeting destined never to occur, as George died the night before they arrived.

Sam lived a long life in Sydney, virtually a generation longer than his parents. He died in 1988, aged 97. He was active, with a clear and independent mind throughout. Indeed, he made several significant and life-changing decisions in his mid-90s. At age 93, he asked the family to buy him underpants, stating that he had never worn any but now felt they would help him keep warm in the winter. In his 96th year, he became a Catholic, stating that 'he wanted to join the family'. Sam had a well-deserved reputation as a magnificent urban gardener, tilling a plot the size of a tennis court in suburban Strathfield. He grew copious vegetables and fruits, but surprisingly little citrus. He preferred the challenge of producing large quantities of Queensland fruits such as mangoes, pawpaw and macadamia nuts. He was Elise's son, with George's yeoman farming genes.

17

Empire's reward

George had two objectives in developing his mandarin. He wanted a variety that would mature early so it could be sent to market in advance of the bulk of the orange citrus crop – the key attribute of 'early'. He also wanted a mandarin that while picked early would have good keeping qualities, so it could be shipped to distant markets and arrive in good condition for the consumer. Fewtrell's Early met both aims and capitalised on the natural advantage of Queensland producers of being able to get fruit to the larger Sydney and Melbourne markets in advance of fruit produced in the southern states. George and other Queensland growers also had some modest success with overseas market penetration. Fewtrell's Early became a recognised citrus variety and, in the years following his death, came to be grown extensively, particularly in Queensland and northern NSW, taking its place in the history of citrus growing in Australia.

While Australia's Aboriginal people were familiar with native citrus plants, European and Asian citrus varieties came to Australia among the cargo of the First Fleet. 'The ports of call – Teneriffe, Rio de Janeiro and the Cape – were all orange growing centres.' Various specimens, both seeds and plants, were taken on board during the month-long stopover in Rio de Janeiro and attracted the particular attention of the Fleet's Commander Arthur Phillip and also its chaplain, Rev. Richard Johnson. It is speculated that their interest was prompted by James Cook's successful encouragement to his sailors to eat limes as an antidote to scurvy, which resulted from dietary deficiencies.

Both Phillip and Johnson were keen to test their horticultural skills in the first years of the colony and the records reveal considerable initial success in advancing the plants. 'On arrival at Port Jackson on Jan. 26, 1788, "the first work performed"', says Frank Bowman, quoting the commemorative *Agricultural Gazette of NSW*, 1901, '"was the planting of seed and plants obtained on the voyage from England at Rio and the Cape of Good Hope, including…oranges of various sorts, both seeds and plants".' It seems likely that mandarins were among the varieties of oranges. Certainly, mandarins were recorded among the citrus varieties in the Sydney Botanic Gardens in 1828.

During the next century, the fortunes of the citrus industry fluctuated significantly. Great uncertainty characterised the industry in the years following World War I. In Queensland and across Australia there was a constant cycle of experimentation with plant varieties, soil types and ultimately production locations. Crop failures were invariably followed by crop bonanzas. However, growers often despaired as they were unable to find markets for the surplus. Such cycles continued into the second half of the 20th century. In short, the industry struggled to survive. Repeated calls were made for export markets to provide an outlet for high-yield years, as a way to underwrite the viability of growers. This was a refrain that had rung out since the 1890s, when it was reported that there was 'keen interest in export to Europe and India'. Building stronger grower associations was another major focus, along with improvements to root stock selection techniques and availability. These items had been on George Fewtrell's agenda, but it seemed the challenges were ongoing.

George's mandarin certainly had its advocates among growers and consumers. In 1935, one North Queensland correspondent to a newspaper gardening column noted the variety's 'rather pleasant taste, not possessed by other varieties', which 'makes the Fewtrell rather easy to distinguish'. The review went on to advocate that 'a little more manure, cow preferably, could be used after pruning and that may bring out more clearly the distinct flavour Fewtrell's Early possesses'.

By the 1940s, one nursery outlet extolled it as 'not a new variety but one of the very best – thin skin, sweet and heavy cropper'. Another positive was its resistance to some common citrus diseases. However, on the negative side, some considered it had too many seeds and others believed that its tendency to crop on alternate years (not uncommon for citrus at the time) was a disadvantage for growers.

In the 1930s, Queensland invested heavily in the development of a citrus budwood scheme, as a way to provide growers with ready supplies of quality-assured plant stock. The Fewtrell's Early mandarin was among the approved varieties covered by this scheme and the variety was also readily available through recognised nurseries in NSW. It became increasingly clear that, to survive, the industry needed more than just reformed grower organisations and export markets. Constant experimentation and research to develop varieties best suited to Australian soils and most suitable for particular export markets would be critical. The gradual move from smaller coastal orchards to broadacre production inland from the range, also contributed to varietal development decisions. Competition seemed particularly intense among the few varieties recognised as 'early'. Citrus expert Frank Bowman listed the prominent early varieties as Imperial, Unshiu, Fewtrell and Clementine. It seemed likely that, in commercial terms, not all would survive.

During the 1930s and 1940s, NSW emerged as the leading citrus producer, with a major focus in the areas of the Cumberland Plain west of Sydney, the foothills of the Blue Mountains and on the Central Coast around Gosford. Entrepreneurial nurserymen, particularly in Sydney's west, began producing abundant stock of many sorts of fruit trees and looked far afield for markets. Shipping records for the late 1930s reveal regular shipments of citrus fruit to markets in Europe and other destinations, including the Punjab. This trade was obviously attracting interest on the subcontinent. One prominent grower, Mr G.B. McKee of Ermington, in Sydney's west, claimed to have consigned 20–30,000 citrus trees to various overseas destinations in a

20-year period immediately following the Great War. A press report at the time noted that 'India is a large user of these trees and they are said to flourish in almost all parts of that country.'

Another leading Sydney grower, Fred Spurway from Brush Farm in Dundas, was reported to have despatched 6,000 citrus trees to India in July 1936. The Spurway nursery had reportedly sent large consignments annually to India in this period. Certainly the *Sydney Daily Commercial News and Shipping List* reported a consignment of five crates of citrus trees being despatched for the Punjab on the P&O *Strathnaver*, which left Sydney on 11 July 1936. It seems that the nursery growers had perfected a shipping technique that enabled plants to withstand voyages of up to six weeks and still thrive on planting. 'The trees' were 'carefully packed for shipment and stripped of their leaves to enable them to withstand the sea voyage.' In addition to India, trees were successfully landed in other destinations, including the US, Argentina and China. By 1940 the Queensland Department of Agriculture and Stock had greatly increased its budwood stock development and was also having success at exporting 'some thousands of trees to…other countries'.

George Fewtrell had answered the Empire's call for yeoman farmers by coming to Queensland in 1874. While he was developing his orchards in Palmwoods, the Empire was also very busy elsewhere, in what was then known as British India and was destined, in 1947, to become the independent states of India and Pakistan. As one observer of British India has noted, '…the period of British rule seemed to be one not only of relative political peace and stability, but also of vigorous economic growth', adding, the 'process of agricultural expansion was extensive' and its impacts were notable in certain areas, marking out 'the Punjab from other provinces of British India as a "beneficiary" of colonial rule'.

Whereas George ventured to Queensland to do the Empire's bidding, now the Empire would return the favour. In the early 1900s, George was an industry leader urging growers to form larger associations to better develop and market their produce and represent their interests. In 1934, the British administration, through the offices of the Department of Agriculture, urged citrus growers of the rich Punjab region to form a central organisation of their own. The following year, the Punjab Provincial Co-operative Fruit Development Board was established, an organisation that would play an absolutely crucial role in the development of the region's citrus industry. The board approached its task comprehensively. Drawing on the success of broadacre citrus production in the US, its vision was expressed as 'our cherished dream of converting the land of the five rivers into California of India'.

One key driving factor was the need to produce sufficient crops to feed the populations of the emerging India and Pakistan – this would later translate into the objective 'The Punjab requires one million tons of fruit per annum.' A further consideration was the increasing focus on diet improvement and the need to ensure appropriate intakes of minerals and vitamins, of which vitamin C was a critical element. Its readily available source was citrus. Underpinning these aspirations was a range of initiatives, including the exhaustive experimentation and selection of varieties of citrus best suited to the climate and soils.

Testing of various citrus plants began in the late 1930s and selected varieties were progressively introduced. Analysis of performance centred on standard factors, such as suitability to the local climate and soils, yield, fruit quality, tree vigour and the regularity of fruit bearing. One other factor that needed assessment was the susceptibility of plants to sunburn in a very hot climate, which was a particular problem in the Canal Colonies, a network of irrigation canals that the British administration constructed in parts of the Punjab. At some point, probably early in the 1940s, Fewtrell's Early mandarin was added to the list of varieties to undergo extensive testing that would extend over several years.

Throughout this time, Fewtrell's Early remained a prominent variety of mandarin in Australia, grown particularly in Queensland and

NSW. No record has been found of any exchange between Australian and British or Indian officials for specimens of the variety to be sent from Australia. However, given the quantities involved in the various commercial consignments over several years, it seems highly likely that the Fewtrell's Early mandarin was included among trees exported to the Punjab in the late 1930s or early 1940s. Indian and Pakistan records have always referred (inaccurately) to Fewtrell's Early as originating from NSW. However, such confusion would have been understandable given the likely source of the trees, via exports from Sydney.

The export of tree stock was curiously at odds with the perennial drive to build export markets for Australian grown citrus fruit. The Australian citrus industry continued its stuttering progress for much of the period between the wars, characterised by expansion, over-development, readjustment and attempts at stabilisation. While overall the industry grew (it produced 5.2 million bushels of product in the five years before World War II, compared with two million bushels in a similar period before World War I), consistent, reliable and profitable export markets proved largely elusive. A national conference of the industry, convened in July 1945 by the federal Minister for Post War Reconstruction, undertook to put new energy into expanding the industry, including providing opportunities for returning servicemen and building export markets to deliver useful returns to growers.

Just as on the subcontinent, the suitability of varieties to meet emerging needs was being assessed. In the Australian context, the focus was on the move to broadacre orchards on the western side of the Great Dividing Range, and rationalising the varieties within specific market categories. Eventually, Fewtrell's Early lost out as the preferred fruit in the strategically important early market category. George Fewtrell's mandarin began to be phased out of Australian orchards and within a decade or so would be virtually unobtainable on the local market.

In the Punjab, however, the story was very different. Fewtrell's Early emerged from the assessment process as a clearly preferred variety for the region. In 1950, the Punjab Fruit Development Board announced that both the Kinnow and Fewtrell's Early were the mandarin varieties 'recommended to fruit growers'. It went on to state that in view of their attributes 'these two varieties will revolutionise the Sangtra cultivation of the province and particularly in the canal colony districts'. The July 1951 edition of the *Punjab Fruit Journal* reported on the trials and selection recommendations for various fruits that had been conducted over the previous decade. The Kinnow was ranked the top sangtra (mandarin), followed by Fewtrell's Early. The two varieties complemented each other, Fewtrell's was an early variety and the Kinnow a later seasonal crop. A later analysis reported in January of 1973 that '...Fewtrell's Early has been found to be an ideal early mandarin for the plains of north India'.

George was a stalwart of Queensland yeoman farmers, brought in to develop the land and industry. The output of his Shropshire-inspired work on the coastal ranges of south-east Queensland was significant, but George's mandarin was to make an even bigger contribution to the Empire in India and Pakistan. His approach was always to have an eye on the bigger picture, but it is unlikely that even he could have foreseen the scope of his legacy, which continues to this day.

18

Identity then and now

In the scope of history, George and Elise made their contributions to the Australian story and moved on. Their family, of course, respects and remembers their roles. Their community honours those roles in the customary manner: a community plaque and a street named for them. George's contribution to the citrus industry is recorded in some ways, but forgotten in others – unfairly so, as it was significant in several respects. Even his legacy achievement, Fewtrell's Early mandarin, is now remembered by only the oldest of industry identities. It is no longer available commercially in Australia, although some trees survive in the NSW Citrus Arboretum at Dareton, in the south of the state. Its resurgence in India and Pakistan has been known only to a few Australian agricultural experts and to his family for only a decade or so. Its misspelling and mistaken origin, NSW instead of Queensland, only highlight the transitoriness of fame and identity.

It is not the longevity of achievement that marks us, rather the significance and impact of the lives lived at the time. Both Elise and George walked paths that were honourable and generous. As such, they add a fragment of colour and texture to the broader mosaic of Australian humanity. They were British and German, but became Australian. That is a journey all immigrants are destined to take. It is also a journey that the country itself, and its people, are embarked upon.

Australia's second prime minister, Alfred Deakin described himself as an 'independent Australian Briton'. A successor and bearer of the same office during much of the World War I, Billy Hughes, was even more specific:

A man may be a very loyal and devoted adherent to and worshipper of, the Empire, and still he may be a very loyal and patriotic Australian all the time.

These views were the accepted identity rubric for most of the first 20 years of Federation. They were symbolised in the design of the Australian flag – Britain in the land of the Southern Cross.

Young George's war may have been against his mother's people, but it also prompted conflict with his father's people. The chronicler of Australia's war, official historian Charles Bean, grew increasingly critical of the prosecution of the war by the British generals, under whose command Australia's troops served. For Bean, the toll of the French battlefields, particularly Passchendaele, marked a low point. Passchendaele is acknowledged as the costliest engagement in a war of horrendous human carnage, with 38,000 Australians either killed, wounded or missing. Bean was contemptuous of the incompetence of many British generals. Later, he would write dismissively of 'the extraordinary British method of choosing men not by their capacity but by their "breeding" or act of birth'. He considered such a system to be the blight of all British institutions.

> The real cause is the social system of England, or the distorted relic of the early middle ages which passes for a system: the exploitation of the whole country for the benefit of a class…

He was appalled that the vigorous youth of Australian manhood was sacrificed on such an altar. These views were widely shared among senior Australian military personnel and were unlikely to have been disputed by the soldiers in the field who carried out their orders. The experiences in the trenches of France and Belgium led directly to pressure for Australians to be under Australian command. A small but significant shift in the perception that Australian interests would always coincide with those of Britain.

The war had tempered the loyalty of Australians to Britain in two senses of the word: in some cases it hardened the imperial consciousness; in others it had moderated that consciousness, even replaced it, with a new awareness of nationalism.

In the 20 years leading to federation and in the years before the war, national identity was seen through the prism of Empire. It was the Deakinite interpretation that persisted, even in the wake of the great achievement that marked the nation building of federation. But following the war there began to be signs of a slow evolution, a refinement in understanding and appreciation. It was the beginning of a process that would stop and start throughout the remainder of the 20th century and continues even today.

In his near 40 years in the country, George was an archetype of the Deakinite construct of national identity. His awareness of nationhood was through the frame of Empire. Australia had presented George with a larger, more satisfying context in which to make his contribution to British society and the Empire. His contributions to nation-building were significant in their own right, focused on community, industry and state. His interests and engagements integrated him into the emerging nationalism, which was subtle and largely undemonstrative. It needed time to grow and emerge slowly from the lived experience of the people and place, and the achievements of the communities they were building.

George would have wanted Australian nationhood to succeed and take its place in the world. Indeed, there was a touch of one-upmanship in his aspirations to export his very own mandarin, bearing his name, back to his homeland. He sought to champion his new home within the global reach of the British Empire. He would have been chuffed to know that his mandarin became a significant food source for millions of the Empire's people. He would have recognised that Australia had given him opportunities that English society, based on Bean's 'distorted relic of the early middle ages', would have denied him.

On the other hand, Elise was on a different journey of national and self-identity. Her formal identity was 'assigned' to her at various stages of her life, whether due to national conflict or as a consequence of marriage, which in turn changed her name and her nationality at the sound of a gun or the stroke of a pen. While she was a happy participant in the formation of the community of Palmwoods, and indeed the contributor of a family of young Australians to that nation, she retained seemingly much of the culture of her homeland. Just as a modern-day citizenship ceremony may endow a migrant with a new national identity, there remains beyond that the journey of the heart, mind and soul, each of which must make their own passage through stages of accommodation, contentment and commitment.

For Elise, it is likely that contentment came fully when she lived to see her children grow up in peace and come of age in this land. While its surroundings may to her still have seemed foreign in some ways, her children saw them instinctively as 'home'. Although Elise became British by virtue of her marriage to George, it was not something that had any particular meaning for her – no sentimental memories, or a well from which to draw context and strength. For her, the process was longer. Moving through accommodation and contentment to commitment required time. She needed time to come to terms with the new and resolve what was leading the dance – memory or the new realities. In this sense, the experience of Elise is more akin to the journeys experienced by migrants in today's multicultural Australia. The past was of value, heritage was worthy of respect, but the commitment was to the future and the place she now called 'home'.

There is a compelling quality about the resolute braveness of those who made the decision to journey from Europe to the Australian colonies. Such decisions speak of a radical earnestness, a powerful force that inspired people to launch into the unknown, to confront the risks and imponderables, in the search for a better life and prospects. Such decisions could only ever be partly informed. They also required, as in the case of both Elise and George, a commitment to work hard and a preparedness to both enjoy and endure the results. Ultimately, a focus on the future meant that those results would also involve the building of a new nation out of a foreign terrain and shared effort.

As the records of the period show, it was not just individual settlers who were adjusting to the new. The outbreak of war brought different challenges and experiences for both the state and commonwealth governments of the federation. They had to devise new formulations and reach common understandings for such basic elements of statecraft as a declaration of war. However, by far the greatest identity challenge was for those who, ironically, possessed the strongest sense of Australian authenticity – the Aboriginal people. Their long lived experience of the land and their profound connection with place meant that in the Sunshine Coast hinterland, as elsewhere, their identity was synonymous with their land. It was a fixture of the firmament, something to be worked with, not conquered and refashioned.

The tragedy was that the settler society was in the process of destroying that identity, largely rejecting it deliberately, without questioning or understanding – seemingly an inevitable outcome of British settlement. While white society was adjusting its concepts of place and home to account for a different physical environment, the remnant knowledge and authentic identity that grew organically from that place was being slowly smothered as a last stage in the war of the frontier. Sadly, in the colonial mindset there was little thought that the two cultures could exist side by side, let alone prevail together, perhaps ultimately to engage or even entwine.

Undeniably, George and Elise were part of this occupation. There is nothing to suggest that they played any role that was overtly aggressive or offensive. Nonetheless, in historical terms they were part of the dispossession process – part of the required phalanx of white settler farmers whom the Queensland government had engineered as literal openers of the soil, the first wave of a 'civilising' western culture. George's frequent mantra 'that the land be thrown open for selection' was in a real sense a call for the completion of the dispossession campaign. It was a passionate call that the authorities, in effect, speed up implementation of the 'bring them in' part of the policy that complemented the 'run them out' phase. George was articulating the white community's desire to finish the dispossession it had begun and the reinforcement of white, Western and essentially British values and lifestyle.

An abiding memory I have is of my grandfather, Sam, speaking in later life of those times and how Aboriginal people would roam the district, taking with them farming and other implements. His words, expressed in a gentle tone, have stayed with me ever since: 'They were thieving so-and-sos.' In reality of course, it was not the Aboriginal people who had done the thieving, rather the white settler farmers and the authorities under whose patronage they acted.

There is no doubt that George and Elise set out on an honourable endeavour to be a pioneering settler family. The fact remains that they were part of the historical instruments of the Queensland colonial authorities at the time, to implement fully the 'run them out and bring them in' policy. Their moment in history meant that they confronted this reality, which arguably is appreciated today in far starker terms than it was at the time. While they may not have been responsible for the dispossession, we, their descendants, do share a responsibility to take steps in our time to restore that identity within the framework of modern Australia and to redress the impacts of that dispossession.

For a brief moment in the early 1840s, there was the opportunity to take a different road, to construct a different Australia. Essentially, the Bunya Proclamation was motivated by a desire to respect the significance that particular land and locations held for Aboriginal people, to protect those areas and retain ongoing access to them for Aboriginal people. Whether deliberately or capriciously, the Bunya Proclamation presented a chance for Aboriginal people to live alongside white settlers, sharing the land, with the opportunity for a broader respectful engagement and understanding between cultures, of the type to which Tom Petrie had been invited and embraced.

It was obviously too much to hope for. It was a statement of recognition which could not withstand the juggernaut of dispersal and removal that informed all other aspects of official policy. But if it could have been sustained, it just might have been possible to negotiate a different Australian compact. Such negotiation would have required all to reconsider the boundaries of their concepts of identity and land ownership.

Governor Gipps's Bunya Proclamation, expressing that moment of opportunity, also stands as a poignant echo of the terms of the commission given to his predecessor and first governor Arthur Phillip. That warrant read, in part

> You are to endeavour by every means to open an intercourse with the natives, and to conciliate their affections, enjoining all our subjects to live in amity and kindness with them, and if any of our subjects shall wantonly destroy them or give them any unnecessary interruption in the exercise of their several occupations, it is our will and pleasure that you do cause such offenders to be brought to punishment.

The Bunya Proclamation, which was intended to protect the Bunya grounds and Aboriginal access to them, was thoroughly consistent with these instructions. The war of the frontier that raged around the Bunya lands was completely at odds with those instructions. How different might have been the Australian compact with its Aboriginal people had Phillip's instructions been carried out faithfully, or indeed if the Bunya Proclamation had endured in the face of the rapacious surge of colonial development and mastery.

In the 70 or so years that had passed since Phillip first took up his post, much had occurred that was inconsistent with the crown's instructions. But it was not just the lack of compliance by Colonial Office representatives that accounted for the change. The granting of colonial self-government to the Queensland people effectively hastened the proclamation's rejection. Notwithstanding the objectives of the Crown, the people's representatives were only too keen to endorse the full effects of the 'run them out and bring them in' approach. The Bunya Proclamation was too radically at odds with an entrenched settlement culture to be sustained.

When in 2015 Aboriginal leader Noel Pearson wrote of the plurality of identities that exist in modern society, he dreamt of an opportunity of mutual recognition and respect that would see Aboriginal people moving between two worlds, 'the aboriginal world and the wider world'. That was part of the vision of the Bunya Proclamation. It stands today as the glimpse of a future Australia that was snuffed out before it could begin. It remains, however, an authentic Australian identity that still beckons.

The plurality of identities, to which Pearson referred, lies at the centre of the modern multicultural Australia – layers of identity, derived from earlier times and places that embrace the whole of the individual. At its heart is a sense of identity that evolves and is enriched by Aboriginal people and those who continue to come and make their own contributions. In this is the richness of Australia's human story.

Notes

Introduction

'Commercial citrus is thought to originate in south-east Asia, among what are now the modern-day states of India, Pakistan and China': the family *Rutaceae* (order Sapindales) is widely distributed with centres of diversity in southern Africa and Australia (Bayer et al. 2009). Commercial citrus are derived from wild species indigenous to the sub-Himalayan tract, China and western Malesia. (Email advice from Australian citrus expert, Dr Pat Barkley.)

'Two varieties dominate, Kinnow (the most common and sourced originally from the US) and Fewtrell from Australia': in both Pakistan and India, the name of the mandarin is often misspelt as Feutrell's Early, instead of Fewtrell's Early.

1: 'I am of Shropshire, my shins be sharp'

'...my shins be sharp': *The Folklore of Shropshire*, p. 36) – an old saying dating back to the 16th century. 'Sharp shins' is a reference to quick-footed and quick-witted.

'a Shropshire mon is nivver lost if he con see the Wrekin': *The Folklore of Shropshire*, p. ix.

'As soon, however, as gardeners picked out individual plants ...': Charles Darwin, *The Origin of Species, The Illustrated Edition*, (from the chapter 'Variation under Domestication'), p. 48.

'...species are not set in stone but to use his word are "plastic"': ibid., p. 21.

'the principle, namely the cumulative power of selection, by which good breeders succeed': *Ask the Beasts*, p. 48.

'...born to Samuel and Maria Fewtrell in 1842 or 43...': George's tombstone states that he was 71 when he died in 1914. The obituary in the *Brisbane Courier* of 11 September 1914 stated his age as 72.

'Servant men, stand up for your wages...': *The Folklore of Shropshire*, p. 177.

'The Standard wage level for farm labourers in southern Shropshire in 1872 was 9 shillings per week': *Domesday Book: 1750–1875, A History of the county of Shropshire: Vol. 4: Agriculture (1989)*, pp. 168–231.

'the government of Queensland was specifically seeking agricultural workers, genuine "yeoman farmers"...': *The Macquarie*

Dictionary defines yeoman as 'British, a countryman, especially one of some social standing, who cultivates his own land; Yeomanry, relating to or befitting a yeoman, sturdy; reliable.'

2: A smooth passage

'Figures on 19th-century migration from European countries...': *Emigration from Europe 1815–1930*.

'Those granted free passage were required to pay £1...': *Handbook for Emigrants to Queensland, Australia*.

'the road seems so clear to success and fortune in Queensland': report of lecture on Queensland given to emigrants by the ship's surgeon, Dr. Concanon, *The Winefred Marvel*, edition No. 12 of 20 March 1875;

'I got into work as soon as we landed in Brisbane in the depot...': *The Winefred Marvel, Supplementary Number*, produced on board the *Winefred* during her voyage from London to Brisbane – Letters from young men in Queensland: from Andrew Gurdler, formerly of Uxbridge, September 5 1874. This was the second voyage to Brisbane of the *Winefred*. George Fewtrell had sailed on the *Winefred*'s earlier voyage to Brisbane.

'It was at this stage of the journey that many an emigrant ship resembled a floating "rag-fair"': *Australia Visited and Revisited*, p. 4.

'The noon formalities, involving the captain and one or two of the Mates...': *The Long Farewell*, p. 15.

'The *Winefred* Marvel – the pride of the Empire...was immortalised by one passenger': The *Winefred* Marvel, produced on board the *Winefred* during her voyage from London to Brisbane, No. 2, Tuesday December 29, 1874, p. 12.

'Labour is wanted, employment is offered...': *Handbook for Emigrants to Queensland, Australia*.

3: The yeoman finds his bearings

'Deniehy...envisage[d] what one observer has described as 'an Australian community of independent yeoman farmers': *Our First Republicans: Lang, Harpur, Deniehy*, p. 11.

'We consider the Small Settler a very important personage.': ibid., p. 162.

'...the state population increasing from 30,000 in 1861...': *The Frontier – A pictorial history of Queensland to 1920*, pp. 3–4.

'Ultimately Queensland by the early 1880s, would have the most multicultural society of all the Australian colonies': *A History of Queensland*, pp. 89, 131.

'Land is cheap because the struggle required to make it useful is severe': *Australia and New Zealand*, pp. 178–180.

'The PAFSOA had begun in Victoria in the 1860s as an association of Protestant interests opposed to attempts by Catholics "to get introduced into our National School curriculum the dogmas of the Roman Church'": early history of PAFSOA, document received from E.J. Richardson, Grand Secretary, Friendly Societies Project, Documents Z87/Box 63, Noel Butlin Archives Centre, Australian National University, Canberra.

'At its heart PAFSOA was "… essentially loyal and patriotic and our vow of loyalty to the Protestant Crown of England was honoured by our members"': The History and Progress of the Protestant Alliance Friendly Society of Australasia, Grand Council of Queensland 1876–1976, p. 27, Documents Z87/Box 63, Noel Butlin Archives Centre, Australian National University, Canberra.

4: A woman from Schleswig-Holstein

'In earlier times, the Elbe spread extensively across the lowlands and Kellinghusen': *850 Jahre Kellinghusen an der Stör*, p. 23 ff.

'The town census of 1860 records that house number 17…': census records obtained by the author from the Kellinghusen town historian, Richard Kolang, in 2001.

'Like many towns in the German Confederation of the time…': *850 Jahre Kellinghusen an der Stör*, p. 33 ff.

5: A very difficult passage

'For a time there were restrictions on males, aged between six and 40, leaving Germany': *A Norwegian Waltz*, p. 32.

'One study of the sailing vessels departing from Hamburg for Queensland…': study by Helen Woolcock as cited in *A Norwegian Waltz*, p. 30.

'Catherina identified as passenger 110, Carl as 111…': *Emigrants from Hamburg to Australia: 1877*, p. 7.

'Elise and Catherina 'hemstitched pillowcases and sheeting…': *One Way Ticket*, p. 56.

'…it was horrid, and even indecent for decent married people to be herded together like beasts…': *The Long Farewell*, p. 102.

'the later emigrants fared worse than did the convicts': ibid., p. 1.

'I was awakened this morning by a poor woman laying her trembling hand on my shoulder…': diary of Mrs Hinshelwood, ibid., p. 165.

'Funerals at sea involved a minimum of procedure…': ibid., p. 196.

'Ellen McConachie, who endured a similar fate on a voyage in 1882 wrote': Wilson family history in *The Exiles of Peel Island*, p. 32.

'Elise was hit by a barrel that had come loose and she was thrown down a companionway': companionway is a nautical term for the space or shaft occupied by the steps leading down from the deck to a cabin, or the steps themselves, *Macquarie Dictionary*.

'…she (Elise) was a very timid, little person and…': comment from Marie Krebbs, quoting her mother, Catherina Kuskopf, on the loss of Elise's baby on the voyage out, as cited in *One Way Ticket*. p. 56.

'The role of the surgeon involved…': *The Long Farewell*, p. 167.

'Come on deck and smell the land!': ibid., p. 215.

7: Quarantine and other trials

'The quarantine station had been built on a bluff on the south/east corner. It had received its first ship in 1873 and a further 23 ships would be directed there': *The Exiles of Peel Island*, pp. 13, 47.

'The facilities were elementary, consisting of only three buildings…'; extract from 'The Week' of 1 January 1876, as recorded in *The Exiles of Peel Island*, p. 14.

'During the period in quarantine "linen and clothing was washed and boiled numerous times. The ship was fumigated and refitted with new equipment"': ibid., p. 18.

'Those who died were at least afforded a burial on shore, in a small area about 600 metres from the other facilities. In 1877 it had already become the last resting place of 10…': Extract from 'The Week' of 1 January 1876, as recorded in *The Exiles of Peel Island*, p. 17.

'On the morning of 1 August 1877 Swedish sailor Charles Larss appeared in the Water Police Court charged with…': Records of Queensland Water Police Court, Queensland State Archives, Item 6301 Dispositions and Minutes Book, pp. 383–389 and 394–97, CPS1/AW134 and SRS6301/1/3.

8: Starting to 'butty' in Homestead 4171

'Acting on his own advice, Peter Kuskopf moved his family north to Merriman Flat (later Palmwoods) in late 1881 or early 1882': *One Way Ticket*, p. 57; *The Palmwoods Story* ('The First Settlers') states that 'In 1881 these three families, connected by marriage, came to Palmwoods.'

'These two family groups, along with Momme and Christine Bendixen (Peter Kuskopf's youngest sister) were the original settlers in what became the township of Palmwoods': *The Palmwoods Story* ('The First Settlers').

'In December 1883, George submitted a formal application': Queensland Archives, Item ID.35681, LAN/AG146; PRV9882/1/6035.

'The land held by George was subsequently reduced': Queensland Archives, Item ID.35681, LAN/AG146; PRV9882/1/6035.

'to butty': *The Folklore of Shropshire*, p. 149.

'The wedding took place on a Friday': ibid., p. 152.

'Nine per cent of immigrants to Queensland were German': *The Call of the Land*, p. 90.

'By 1891 a third of the German emigrants to Australia resided in Queensland': *The Call of the Land*, p. 149.

'Kuskopf was at this time moving into his latest and last business venture': *One Way Ticket*, p. 66.

'During the 1880s and early 1890s Queensland was afflicted with major natural disasters…': *The Call of the Land*, p. 129.

9: 'This land is mine: this land is me'

'This land is mine: this land is me': title of song by Paul Kelly.

'In November 1868, Cobb & Co. had earlier established a service from Brisbane to Gympie': Fred Fink Collection, Early History of the Maroochy District, Vol, 6.1, p. 5.

'The deed granting the land for Homestead Selection 4171': Queensland Archives, Item ID.35681, LAN/AG146; PRV9882/1/6035.

'It was a marker of the *terra nullius* world view that prevailed': from the Latin 'the land of no one'; the prevailing legal doctrine for the possession of land in the Australian colonies, until overturned in 1992 by the High Court of Australia in the Mabo case.

'Land "was in fact seething with an ancient rhythm": *Conspiracy of Silence*, p. xxiv.

'The name "Dalla" is from the term in the local language for the staghorn, which flourishes in the rainforest. "Nalbo" is…': *A Submerged History*, p. 7.

'the great Bunya Festival of Baroon': several sources, including *Sunshine Coast Aboriginal Culture before the White Man* and the Fred Fink Collection Vol. 1, p. 3.4a.

'In explaining the highly organised and respectful manner in which such festivals were conducted, one early writer made the observation that "These people set us an example that with all our boasted civilisation we might well follow"': *Making Maroochy*, p. 5, citing E. Thorne, *The Queen of the Colonies*, p. 24.

'Tom Petrie later described aspects in his *Reminiscences*': Tom Petrie's *Reminiscences*, p. 22.

'Young Tom Petrie…and Christopher Rolleston…advocated that the area be set aside': Fred Fink Collection, Vol. 1, p. 3.1, citing *In the Wake of the Raftsmen*, p. 3; and *Conspiracy of Silence*, p. 22.

'Governor Gipps took particular interest in the matter and during an extended visit to Brisbane accepted the advice': *Warrior*, p. 68.

'However, the poisoning of a large number of Aboriginals on a property at Kilcoy, to the north of the Bunya Baroon in January 1842': *Conspiracy of Silence*, pp. 83–84.

'More than 100 years later this event would be described in a semi-official account as "the 'death pudding' of arsenic, a trap which took seventy native lives, for the theft of half a bag of flour…"': *Triumph in the Tropics*, p. 184.

'Noted Dalla warrior Dundalli provides a case study of how strict and honourable observance of cultural lore and practice could lead to a series of attacks…': *Warrior*, pp. 57–88.

'In chronicling the story of Dundalli, Libby Connors has identified how "according to Gubbi Gubbi oral history Dundalli was a kooringal…"': ibid., pp. 150 ff.

'Certainly the period between 1843 and 1855 is seen by Aboriginal sources as a time of active resistance – a 'Black War' – ': *Chronological Summary – Sunshine Coast Aboriginal Culture before the White Man*, pp. 1–2.

'It is worth noting that Cilento's semi-official account of the times, published in 1959 does not hesitate to call it a "Black War" that "flared after the great bunya festivals of 1841 and 1844"': *Triumph in the Tropics*, p. 184. Cilento goes on to state that Aboriginals 'for twenty years from 1842…maintained their attack', p. 185.

'Their role was "to clear the frontier of white settlement of troublesome aboriginals" (and other subsequent Native Police activities)': *Sunshine Coast Aboriginal Culture before the White Man*, pp. 6–7.

'Commissioner Rolleston had his own reservations as to the extent the Bunya Proclamation could adequately protect the area. In 1851 he raised his concerns with the Chief Commissioner…': *Conspiracy of Silence*, p. 22.

'The most notable of these occurred at the aptly named Murdering Creek': An evaluation of knowledge of the massacre of Murries at Murdering Creek, Sunshine Coast.

'Another massacre is reported in Aboriginal testimonies as having occurred at Eudlo': *Sunshine Coast Aboriginal Culture before the White Man*, pp. 2–3.

'This area is heavily timbered country with defined sections of open grasslands that even today bear characteristics that Bill Gammage has catalogued…': *The Biggest Estate on Earth*, pp. 1–100.

'…it was also "'the intent of the Almighty we should cultivate the ground"': *Warrior*, p. 46.

'These were the days when aborigines roamed the district in groups of 50 to 100….': handwritten record by Marie Krebs of life on the Kuskopf property in the early 1880s, Fred Fink Collection Section 52, Vol. 6.1.

'Tom Petrie would later reflect, "How different a native was in those old times!…"': Tom Petrie's *Reminiscences*, p.178.

10: A community emerges

'Kuskopf, Bendixen and Fewtrell names figured prominently': *The Palmwoods Story*.

'In 1905 George, although no longer a parent, was elected to the school committee and subsequently to the role of chair:' *Nambour Chronicle*, 17 February 1905.

'George approached other denominations': recollection of personal conversation with Samuel Markus Fewtrell.

'George later served as a local preacher at the church, conducting services on a rostered basis and organising the Sunday School for instruction of the children. As Superintendent of the Sunday School…': *Nambour Chronicle*, 13 November 1903 and 10 June 1904.

'George Fewtrell and Peter Kuskopf were among those calling for local autonomy': Queensland State Archives, Colonial Secretary Office, Correspondence, Caboolture Divisional Board 1897–1929, COL/014, Letter 95, Petitions 8/1/1890.

'In 1891 the population of the district served by the Maroochy Divisional Board': Early History of the Maroochy District, p. 4, Vol. 6.1, Fred Fink Collection.

'George served two periods as chairman of the board (along with other records of meetings during his tenure on the Board)': Minute Books of Maroochy Divisional Board 1890–1900, held at the Council Archive, Nambour.

'A month earlier he was appointed a Justice of the Peace in the colony of Queensland…': Queensland State Archives, *Supplement to the Queensland Police Gazette*, Vol. xxxv, Saturday 8 January 1898.

11: The yeoman builds a nation

'It contained a large kitchen table (plus most other details regarding the house, property and roles)': sound recording of interview with Samuel Markus Fewtrell, May 1982.

'Palmwoods had an average annual rainfall of 65 inches with 103 days being classified as "wet days"': 'The pineapple soils of the Nambour, Woombye and Palmwoods districts', *Queensland Agricultural Journal*, 1 August 1940, State Library of Queensland.

'George did this by observing and noting varieties that showed promise of the desired qualities and then experimenting with blending those attributes with other robust, well-performing citrus lines': there are no known records of the varieties of citrus grown on the Fewtrell property or used by George Fewtrell in the development of his mandarin. The Fewtrell's Early is said by some agricultural scientists (Australian, Dr Greg Johnson and French Emeritus Professor JM Bové) to likely be 'a natural tangor (mandarin x sweet orange) with Willowleaf as the mandarin parent': see documents cited. A technical description of Fewtrell's Early is recorded in official citrus records as follows: 'Fruit medium-small to medium, sub-globose to broadly obovate, base usually rounded; apex flattened. Rind medium in thickness; moderately adherent but easily peelable at maturity; texture and surface more orange-like than mandarin; colour orange to reddish-orange. Segments numerous (11–14); axis semi-hollow. Flesh orange-coloured; moderately juicy; flavour mild and not distinctive. Seeds numerous. Early in maturity (about like Imperial). Tree of medium vigour, spreading and round-topped, dense, symmetrical, and productive. Strong tendency to alternate bearing, with small fruit in "on-crop" seasons.': *The Citrus Industry, Volume 1 — History, World Distribution, Botany and Varieties*, Chapter 4 'Horticultural Varieties of Citrus' by R.W. Hodgson, p. 515, University of California, Division of Agricultural Services, 1967.

'The right to vote was not something that he had experienced or even expected back in England. Here however, it was his right and an opportunity to participate in the building of his community and country': following electoral reforms in the UK in 1867, the right to vote was extended to some categories of skilled working class men in towns, but remained a system based essentially on property rights. This continued to be the case until reforms in 1918, following the end of the World War I, which gave the vote to all men aged over 21 and all women over the age of 30.

'the "home was open house for those who sought his companionship and help…"': *The Palmwoods Story*, 'The Fewtrells', pp. 9–10.

'In the view of one constitutional expert, he was "the most gifted jurist…"': *The Australian Constitution*, p. 16.

'Queensland voted in favour, but by the narrowest of margin of any state': *A History of Queensland*, p. 141.

'Gympie, the strong mining city to the north of Palmwoods': *Andrew Fisher: Prime Minister of Australia*, p. 92.

'His contributions were described as clear and lucid. He was a man who could put together "a natty speech"': *The Nambour Chronicle*, 14 August 1903 and 23 June 1905.

'That "Queensland nativism"': *From the Frontier*, p. 6.

12: A man with wide horizons

'For example in the mid-1890s the Palmwoods growers introduced a cooperative buying scheme': *Making Maroochy*, p. 63.

'In late 1900 a paper was presented to the Palmwoods Progressive and Industrial Progress Association dealing with the export and packing of citrus fruits:' *Queensland Agricultural Journal*, 1 February 1901, State Library of Queensland.

'George Fewtrell, as the driving force in the Palmwoods Association, was strongly behind such ideas and no doubt took much of this thinking to the Bundaberg conference to which he was a delegate': Fred Fink Collection Vol. 52, 10.1.

'This was done "by packing the fruit in small three dozen cases with an edging of lace paper and a small label bearing the name 'Queensland Mandarins'…"': *Making Maroochy*, p. 57.

'Another variety which has only recently been introduced is one called Fewtrell's Shipping Mandarin and raised by Mr Fewtrell…':

Queensland Agricultural Journal, 1 July 1901, State Library of Queensland.

'...the work of the Conference was entrusted to a body of thoughtful, highly intelligent, practical men': ibid.

'Under the old system all that the Association could do was to consult with others...by bringing them into touch with their neighbours the Association had accomplished something that justified its existence': remarks attributed to George Fewtrell in the *Nambour Chronicle* report of the meeting, Friday 7 December 1906.

'More than 60 years later, a review of the history of the development of fruit marketing in Queensland, concluded...': 'The creation of the Committee of Direction of Fruit Marketing', 1970, *Queensland Heritage*, Vol. 2, pp. 31 ff, State Library of Queensland.

13: Growing and going in all directions

'Aunty Kuskopf, as Catherina was known affectionately in the Fewtrell household...': sound recording of interview with Samuel Markus Fewtrell, May 1982 (held by the author).

'By around 1907 she was effectively bedridden from the damage done years earlier in that storm...': the doctor's notation on Elise's death certificate stated 'bedridden for the last 12 years or so'.

'He remembered her as being an assertive and organised person who would "take charge" and "get on with things". Maria made sure that Sam, despite being the youngest, was an active contributor, although in his mind he ended up doing "all the things the others didn't want to do"': sound recording of interview with Samuel Markus Fewtrell, May 1982.

'To lessen her sense of withdrawal the family organised for a mirror to be placed strategically on an inner wall, facing the window. This gave Elise a perspective of the world outside': ibid., May 1982.

'George had made his will in 1898, when aged 54 and at the height of his involvement in civic and citrus affairs. He nominated his executors as...': Queensland State Archives, Document ID: 2105342, Will No. 584 of 1914.

'In May of 1911 he was acknowledged as a donor to the King George Coronation Presentation Fund...': *Brisbane Courier,* 23 May 1911, p. 5.

'Sam recalled that he often spoke with his mother about Schleswig-Holstein. She would tell him of the uncertainty and fear...': sound recording of interview with Samuel Markus Fewtrell, May 1982.

'In October 1912 the progress of Palmwoods received a major fillip with the auction of "the famous big paddock..."': *The Nambour Chronicle,* 11 October 1912.

'In August 1912, George was elected

a vice president of the Palmwoods Central Progress Association. Several days later he was also elected to the same role with the local branch of the Queensland Farmers Union…': *The Nambour Chronicle*, 7 September 1912.

'In August 1913, George chaired a meeting of the Palmwoods Branch of the QFU, principally devoted to examining the whole of "the platform policy of the Country Liberal Party"': *The Nambour Chronicle*, 15 August 1913.

14: A declaration and a death

'Bismarck had serious misgivings about Wilhelm II, eldest grandson of Queen Victoria. Bismarck had said of his Emperor…': *The Outbreak of World War I*, p .9.

'Within weeks of the Sarajevo shooting the Australian Governor-General, Sir Rohan Munro Ferguson, received a cable from London advising that Australia should "adopt precautionary phase" for war…': Queensland State Archives Historical Studies: Queensland and the declaration of war in 1914.

'The Australian Constitution was (is) silent on the matter of a declaration of war and the prevailing view was that "the creation of a state of war and the establishment of peace necessarily resided in the Sovereign himself as the Head of the Empire"': Queensland State Archives Historical Studies: Queensland and the declaration of war in 1914, quoting Mr Justice Isaacs in the High Court in 1916.

'Adding to the confusion and lack of clarity around the identity of the state as an institution with authority to announce and prosecute a war, the governor-general chose to forward to all state governors the cable he had received from London that stated, "War has broken out with Germany. Send all State Governors"': Queensland State Archives Historical Studies: Queensland and the declaration of war in 1914.

'The potential uncertainty was compounded by a proclamation from the Supreme Court of Queensland, published in the *Queensland Government Gazette* of 31 October 1914, regarding the handling of "Probates and Letters of Administration during the continuance of the War now existing between Great Britain and Germany and Austria-Hungary"': Queensland State Archives, *Queensland Government Gazette, No. 166, 31 October 1914*, pp. 1602–1603.

15: Son of the father, son of the mother

'A first sworn statement, signed by the four executors (minus Elise) used the formulation…': Queensland State Archives, Document ID: 2105342, Will No. 584 of 1914.

'The formulation, in relation to the matter of the nationality of a beneficiary, used in this document was more expansive': Queensland

State Archives, Document ID: 2105342, Will No. 584 of 1914.

'George was deployed to France in June 1916 and saw action in places whose names speak of the hell with which they were associated: Armentiers, Poziers, the Somme until Bullecourt, Messines and Passchadelle': war record of George James Fewtrell, Australian Archives website.

'He stated that since his arrival in France in June 1916, "I don't think that I have had a fair deal from my Platoon officer…"': war record of George James Fewtrell, Trial of Pte. Fewtrell G. J. 15th Bn. AIF. 23/7/18, Australian Archives website.

'While on this visit he was put under some pressure to "forget about" this young woman in Sydney, pregnant and catholic. He could simply stay in Queensland and start another chapter in his life': testimony from Joyce Fewtrell, wife of Sam and Florence's eldest child, Colin. Following the death of his parents, Colin found letters that Sam had written to Florence at the time, promising that he would return and marry her. The letters were later destroyed.

16: Endings without Meetings

'As has been said by one seer, "…the commitment to life, can only come about through letting go of the need to control and accepting the risk of encounter"': *The Unbearable Wholeness of Being*, p. 189.

17: Empire's reward

'The ports of call – Teneriffe, Rio de Janeiro and the Cape – were all orange growing centres.': *A History of Citrus-growing in Australia 1788–1900*, p. 2.

'On arrival at Port Jackson on Jan. 26, 1788, "the first work performed", says Frank Bowman quoting the commemorative *Agricultural Gazette of NSW, 1901*, "was the planting of seed and plants obtained on the voyage from England at Rio and the Cape of Good Hope, including…oranges of various sorts, both seeds and plants"': ibid., p. 2.

'Certainly mandarins were recorded among the citrus varieties in the Botanic Gardens Sydney in 1828': ibid., p. 5.

'This was a refrain that had rung out since the 1890s when it was reported there was "keen interest in export to Europe and India"': ibid., p. 11.

'In 1935 one North Queensland correspondent to a newspaper gardening column noted the variety's "rather pleasant taste, not possessed by other varieties" which "makes the Fewtrell rather easy to distinguish"': *Townsville Daily Bulletin*, p. 9, Tuesday 30 July 1935, http://trove.nla.gov.au/ndp/del/article/62409589.

'By the 1940s one nursery outlet extolled it as "not a new variety but one of the very best – thin skin, sweet and heavy cropper"': The Sunshine Nursery Co. Lismore,

NSW http://trove.nla.gov.au/ndp/del/article/98621018.

'In the 1930s Queensland invested heavily in the development of a Citrus Budwood Scheme as a way to providing growers with ready supplies of quality assured plant stock. The Fewtrell's Early mandarin was among the approved varieties able to be sourced through this scheme': *Queensland Yearbook 1937*, p. 790.

'…and the variety was also readily available through recognised nurseries in NSW': advertisements for the Sunshine Nursery Co. Lismore NSW 28 May 1940 and 11 June 1940, http://trove.nla.gov.au/ndp/del/article/98621018 and http://trove.nla.gov.au/ndp/del/article/98622943

'Citrus expert Frank Bowman listed the prominent early varieties as Imperial, Unshiu, Fewtrell and Clementine. It seemed that not all would survive in commercial terms': *Citrus Growing in Australia*, p. 21.

'Shipping records for the late 1930s reveal regular shipments of citrus fruit to markets in Europe and other destinations, including the Punjab: *Daily Commercial News and Shipping List*, 6 August 1936, p. 6; and NSW Export Manifests, 12 August 1937, p. 1.

'One prominent grower, Mr G.B. McKee of Ermington in Sydney's west claimed to have consigned 20–30,000 citrus trees to various overseas destinations in a twenty-year period immediately following the Great War. A press report at the time noted that "India is a large user of these trees and they are said to flourish in almost all parts of that country"': *Sydney Morning Herald*, 17 September 1936, p. 7: http://nla.gov.au/nla.news-article17279272 .

'Another leading Sydney grower, Fred Spurway from Brush Farm in Dundas, was reported to have despatched 6,000 citrus trees to India in July 1936. The Spurway nursery had reportedly sent large consignments annually to India in this period': *The Cumberland Argus and Fruitgrowers Advocate*, 30 July 1935 - http://nla.gov.au/nla.news-article104692845 .

'By 1940 the Queensland Department of Agriculture and Stock had greatly increased its budwood stock development and was also having success at exporting "some thousands of trees to…other countries"': Report of the Director of Fruit Culture, p. 23 of the Annual Report of the Department of Agriculture and Stock, Queensland Parliamentary Papers for the session of 1940.

'Certainly the Sydney *Daily Commercial News and Shipping List* reported a consignment of five crates of citrus trees being despatched for the Punjab on the P&O *Strathnaver* that left Sydney on 11 July 1936': *Daily Commercial News and Shipping List*, 18 July 1936, p. 6, http://nla.gov.au/ndp/del/printArticleJpg/161428606/3?print-y.

'It seems that the nursery growers had perfected a shipping technique that enabled plants to withstand voyages of up to six weeks and still thrive on planting. "The trees" were "carefully packed for shipment and stripped of their leaves to enable them to withstand the sea voyage". In addition to India, trees were successfully landed in other destinations that included the US, Argentina and China': *Sydney Morning Herald*, 17 September 1936, p. 7: http://nla.gov.au/nla.news-article17279272.

'As one observer of British India has noted, "...the period of British rule seemed to be one not only of relative political peace and stability, but also of vigorous economic growth", adding, the "process of agricultural expansion was extensive" and its impacts were notable in certain areas, marking out "the Punjab from other provinces of British India as a 'beneficiary' of colonial rule"': *The Punjab under Imperialism, 1885–1947*. p. vii.

'Drawing on the success of broadacre citrus production in the US, its vision was expressed as "our cherished dream of converting the land of the five rivers into California of India"': *Punjab Fruit Journal*, April 1947, Vol. XI, No. 42.

'One key driving factor was the need to produce sufficient crops to feed the populations of the emerging India and Pakistan – this would later translate into the objective "The Punjab requires one million tons of fruit per annum"': *Punjab Fruit Journal*, January–April 1948, p. 197.

'While overall the industry grew (it produced 5.2 million bushels of product in the five years prior to World War II, compared with 2 million bushels in a similar period prior to World War I), consistent, reliable and profitable export markets proved largely elusive. A national conference of the industry, convened in July 1945 by the Federal Minister for Post War Reconstruction...': Proceedings of Citrus Industry Conference Canberra 1945, Queensland State Archives, Item 1157268, Series 1208.

'In 1950 the Punjab Fruit Development Board announced that both the Kinnow and Fewtrell's Early were the varieties "recommended to fruit growers". It went on to state that in view of their attributes "these two varieties will revolutionise the Sangtra cultivation of the province and particularly in the canal colony districts": *Punjab Fruit Journal*, April–July 1950, p. 21.

'The July 1951 edition of the *Punjab Fruit Journal* reported on the trials and selection recommendations for various fruits that had been conducted over the previous decade. The Kinnow was ranked the top sangtra (mandarin), followed by Fewtrell's Early. The two varieties complemented each other, Fewtrell's was an early variety and the Kinnow a later seasonal crop': *Punjab Fruit Journal*, July 1951 p. 34.

'A later analysis reported in January of 1973 that "…Fewtrell's Early has been found to be an ideal early mandarin for the plains of north India"': Farmer and Parliament (Farmers Parliamentary Forum), January 1973, p. 19.

18: Identity then and now

'Australia's second prime minister, Alfred Deakin, was quoted as describing himself as an "independent Australian Briton". A successor and bearer of the same office during much of World War I, Billy Hughes would be even more specific': *Lion and Kangaroo*, p. 22.

'It is acknowledged as the costliest engagement of the war, with 38,000 Australians being either killed, wounded or missing': Passchendaele: An almost universal experience, Australian War Memorial website.

'Bean was contemptuous of the incompetence of many British generals. He would later write dismissively of "the extraordinary British method of choosing men not by their capacity but by their 'breeding' or 'act or birth'"': *Bearing Witness*, p. 327.

'The war had tempered the loyalty of Australians to Britain in two sense of the word: in some cases it hardened the imperial consciousness. in others it had moderated that consciousness, even replaced it, with a new awareness of nationalism': *Lion and Kangaroo*, p. 307.

'Governor Gipps's Bunya Proclamation also stands as a poignant reminder of the terms of the commission given to his predecessor and first governor Arthur Phillip. That warrant read…': *The Commonwealth of Thieves*, p. 86.

'When in 2015 Aboriginal leader Noel Pearson wrote of the plurality of identities that exist in modern society he dreams of an opportunity of mutual recognition and respect that would see Aboriginal people moving between two worlds, "the aboriginal world and the wider world"': *A Rightful Place*, pp.36, 31.

Bibliography

Ackerman, Jennifer G., *Chance in the House of Fate: A Natural History of Heredity*, Bloomsbury, London, 2001

Baines, Dudley, 'Emigration from Europe 1815–1930', *New Studies in Economics and Social History*, Cambridge University Press, 1995

Bell, Jeanie (compiler with assistance from Amanda Seed), *Dictionary of the Gubbi-Gubbi and Butchulla languages*, Sunshine Coast Library – Heritage Library, March 1994

Bottoms, Timothy, *Conspiracy of Silence: Queensland's frontier killing times*, Allen & Unwin, Sydney, 2013

Bové, J.M., *Virus and virus-like diseases of citrus in the near east region*, Food and Agriculture Organisation of the United Nations, Rome, 1995, http://wwwfao.org/docrep/U5000E/U5000Eoj.htm#Citrus

Bowman, Frank T., 'A History of Citrus-Growing in Australia 1788–1900', reprinted from *The Citrus News*, July–December 1955, 422 Collins Street, Melbourne

—, *Citrus-Growing in Australia*, Angus & Robertson, Sydney, 1956

Bradford, Fay, *One Way Ticket*, Offspring Publications, Brisbane, 2003

Cilento, Raphael (with Clem Lack), *Triumph in the Tropics, An Historical Sketch of Queensland for the Historical Committee of the Centenary Celebrations Council of Queensland* (Crown Copyright Reserved), Smith & Paterson Pty Ltd, Brisbane, 1959

Domesday Book: 1750–1875, A History of the county of Shropshire: Vol. 4: Agriculture (1989), pp.168–231. URL http://british-history.ac.uk/report.aspx?compid=22844 accessed 1 June 2014

Connors, Libby, *Warrior: a legendary leader's dramatic life and violent death on the colonial frontiers*, Allen & Unwin, Sydney, 2015

Day, David, *Andrew Fisher: Prime Minister of Australia*, Harper Collins, Sydney, 2008

Delio, Ilia, *The Unbearable Wholeness of Being*, Orbis Books, New York, 2013

Evans, Raymond, *A History of Queensland*, Cambridge University Press, 2007

Farmer and Parliament, Journal of the Farmers' Parliamentary Forum, New Delhi, India, Vol. VIII, No. 1, January 1973

Fitzgerald, Ross, *A History of Queensland: From the Dreaming to*

1915, University of Queensland Press, 1982

Fraser, Garth, & Neil McGarvie, *A Short History of the Buderim–Palmwoods Tramway* (condensed version of the book *The Buderim–Palmwoods Tramway*), Buderim–Palmwoods Tramway Incorporated, Buderim, Queensland, 2014

The Fred Fink Research Collection, Heritage Library, Sunshine Coast Council, Nambour, Queensland

Gammage, Bill, *The Biggest Estate on Earth: How Aborigines made Australia*, Allen & Unwin, Sydney, 2011

Gregory, Helen, *Making Maroochy: A history of the land, the people and the Shire*, Boolarong Publications with Maroochy Shire Council, Brisbane, 1991

Handbook for Emigrants to Queensland, Australia, by authority of the Agent-general for the Government of Queensland, London, 1875

Headon, David, & Elizabeth Perkins (eds), *Our First Republicans: Lang, Harpur, Deniehy*, Federation Press, Sydney, 1998

Hetherington, F.W., *Life on an Emigrant Ship – The Winefred Marvel*, Free Emigration Office, Uxbridge, London, 1874/75

Hetherington, Michelle (ed.), *Glorious Days: Australia 1913*, National Museum of Australia Press, Canberra, 2013

Hodgson, R.W., *Horticultural Varieties of Citrus* in *The Citrus Industry, Vol. 1, History, World Distribution, Botany and Varieties*, chapter 4, University of California, Division of Agricultural Services, 1967

Iran Ali, Imran, *The Punjab under Imperialism, 1885–1947*, Princeton University Press, New Jersey, 1988

Johnson, Elizabeth A., *Ask the Beasts: Darwin & the God of Love*, Bloomsbury Publishing, London, 2014

Johnson, Greg, Pakistan Citrus Industry Challenges: Opportunities for Australia-Pakistan collaboration in Research, Development & Extension, Horticulture 4 Development, Citrus Industry Survey and Workshops, Pakistan, July 2006. http://aciar.gov.au/files/node/739/ASLP%20citrus%20scoping%20study%20report.pdf

Johnston, W. Ross, *The Call of the Land" A History of Queensland to the Present Day*, Jacaranda Press, 1982

Jones, Stephen, *A Submerged History*, Stephen Jones, Maleny, Queensland, 1990

Kelly, Pat, & Sim Symons (compilers), *Lost Dreaming: Aspects of Traditional Aboriginal Life of the Coolum District*, Sunshine Coast Library, Local Studies Collection, 1989

Keneally, Thomas, *The Commonwealth of Thieves*, Random House Australia, Sydney, 2005

Kenneally, Christine, *The Invisible History of the Human Race*, Black Inc., Melbourne, 2014

Kerkhove, Ray, *Sunshine Coast*

Aboriginal Culture before the White Man, Foundation for Aboriginal & Islanders Research Action, Brisbane, Sunshine Coast Library, Local Studies Collection, 1986

—, *Aboriginal Nambour*, South Coast Libraries, Local Studies, 2009

Kopittke, Eric & Rosemary (compilers) *Emigrants from Hamburg to Australia: 1877*, Queensland Family History Society Inc., April 2000

Lightfoot, J.L., *An Australia Post and Telecom Australia History: Woombye Post Office,* Telecom Australia, 25 August 1977

Lund, Fredrik Larsen, A Norwegian Waltz, Norwegian Immigration and Settlement in Queensland 1870–1914, Masters Thesis in History, University of Oslo, Department of Archaeology, Conservation and History, submitted April 2012, State Library of Queensland,

MacMillan, Margaret, *The War that ended Peace,* Random House, New York, 2013

Mathew, John, T*wo Representative Tribes of Queensland*, T. Fisher Unwin, London 1910

Mossman, Samuel, & Thomas Bannister, *Australia Visited and Revisited: A Narrative of recent travels and old experiences in Victoria and New South Wales*, Ure Smith, Sydney, 1974 (originally published London, 1853)

Palmer, Roy, *The Folklore of Shropshire*, Logaston Press, Herefordshire, 2004

The Palmwoods Story, an historical magazine produced in conjunction with the Back to Palmwoods Week, 7–14 October 1972

Pearson, Noel, 'A Rightful Place: Race, Recognition and a more complete Commonwealth', *Quarterly Essay*, Issue 55, 2014

Petrie, Constance Campbell, *Tom Petrie's Reminiscences of Early Queensland*, Watson Ferguson & Co, Brisbane, 1904

Postel, Ulf O., *850 Jahre Kellinghusen an der StÖr, Druckhaus KÖthen,* Germany, 1998

Prest, R.L., 'Citrus Culture in Queensland', *Queensland Department of Agriculture Bulletin*, undated

The Punjab Fruit Journal, official quarterly organ of the Punjab Provincial Co-operative Fruit Development Board, Editions from 1938–1952, sourced from Cornell University, New York, USA, via interlibrary loan through the National Library of Australia

Quammen, David, *From so Simple a Beginning: The Four Great Books of Charles Darwin*, Stirling Publishing, New York, 2008

Queensland Journal of Agriculture, Department of Agriculture & Stock, Queensland Government, issues from 1897 to 1919 and 1940 to 1953, State Library of Queensland

Records of Queensland Water Police Court, Queensland Archives, 6301 Deposition and Minute Books, Ps. 383-389 and 394–397,CPS1/AW134 and SRS6301/1/3

Rees, Peter, *Bearing Witness*, Allen & Unwin, Sydney, 2015

Reynolds, Henry, *Frontier: Reports from the edge of White Settlement*, Allen & Unwin, Sydney, 1987

— *This Whispering in Our Hearts*, Allen & Unwin, Sydney, 1998

Robin, Libby, *How a Continent Created a Nation*, UNSW Press, Sydney, 2007

Ross, A.A., 'Citrus Growing in Queensland', *Queensland Agricultural Journal*, 1952

Saunders, Kay, 'Queensland and the declaration of war in 1914', *Historical Studies*, Queensland State Archives, August 2014

Sawer, Geoffrey, *The Australian Constitution*, Australian Government Publishing Service, Canberra, 1975

Shogren, D., 'The creation of the Committee of Direction of Fruit Marketing', *Queensland Heritage*, Vol. 2, No. 5, November 1971

Souter, Gavin, *Lion and Kangaroo: Australia: 1901–1919: The Rise of a Nation*, William Collins, Sydney, 1976

Stevenson, David, *The Outbreak of the First World War: 1914 in Perspective*, Macmillan Press, London, 1997

Strachan, Hew, *The Outbreak of World War I*, Oxford University Press, Oxford, 2004

Tibbitts, Craig, Passchendaele: An almost universal experience, Australian War Memorial website www.awm.gov.au

Trollope, Anthony, *Australia and New Zealand*, George Robertson, Melbourne, 1873

Upcher, Janet, *Changing Countries, Bridging Worlds: The Poetry and Prose of Margaret Scott*, Ginninderra Press, Port Adelaide, 2014

Warner, Di, & Amanda Wilson (compilers), *Cyclone and Flood Survey South East Queensland 1800s–2000*, Sunshine Coast Library, Heritage Library

Waterson, Duncan, & Maurice French, *From the Frontier: A pictorial history of Queensland to 1920*, University of Queensland Press, 1987

Watson, F.J., 'Vocabularies of Four Representative Tribes of South East Queensland', Supplement to *Journal of the Royal Geographic Society of Australasia* (Queensland), No. 34, Vol. XLVIII

Wilkinson, Helen (compiler and editor), *Stories of Palmwoods*, Sunshine Coast Council, 2014

Willmott, W.E., & N.C. Stevens, *Rocks and Landscapes of the Sunshine Coast*, Geological Society of Australia (Queensland Division), Brisbane, 1988

Windolf, John F.P., *An evaluation of knowledge of the massacre of Murries at Murdering Creek, Sunshine Coast*, researched and written for Maroochy Libraries, Heritage Library, Nambour, 2001

Yandina: 125 years 1871–1996, Yandina & District Historical Project Group, August 1996

Thanks and acknowledgements

The stories of George and Elise have fascinated me for most of my adult life. The details passed down through the family were somewhat scant, but always the pathos and courage of Elise in overcoming her trials won my interest and attention. Apart from the fact that George grew citrus and had developed a distinctive variety of mandarin, little else was known of him. Gradually over time, through research and investigation, it was possible to assemble a far more detailed picture of these two pioneer Australians. The more I learned, the more I felt the need to tell their stories to a wider audience, for they were stories that deserved to be known.

The question that always emerged was how best to tell the story. After some false starts, it gradually became clear that I might best tell their stories in the social context of their times, in both their northern hemisphere and Australian settings. In this way, I could consider them as granular history, set in the context of the broader historical narratives, with scope for some reflection on their lives and responses to the challenges they faced.

My long-term interest in George and Elise was shared by my older sister, Barbara Dobinson, perhaps because, as the eldest grandchildren who lived for some years with our paternal grandparents Sam and Florence, we had a stronger connection to, and a longer relationship with, our grandfather Sam. Having resolved the approach and embarked on the task, I recalled very clearly Barbara's words – 'this is a very ambitious project' – as conveying an appropriate mixture of caution and encouragement. It is the latter that has dominated the support I have received throughout from Barbara and the wider family. Barbara also provided invaluable advice on narrative style and an assured reference service on dates and details of such matters as births, deaths and marriages.

The various elements of the story involved different research and analysis challenges. I am greatly indebted to a number of people and institutions, including

Gerhard Meixner for German language translation and cultural and historical advice;

Richard Kolang, Kellinghusen town historian;

Joan Bryers of Nambour and District Historical Museum;

Wendy McMullin, Palmwoods resident and member of Nambour Genealogical Society;

Maude Shelden, daughter of George James Fewtrell;

Librarians of the Sunshine Coast Library Service, particularly the Nambour Library, the Fred Fink Research Collection and the archive of Maroochy Shire Council records;

Librarians of the State Library of Queensland;

Archivists of the Queensland State Archives, in particular Jane Wassell for assistance with records on probate and wills, including liaison with the Library of the Supreme Court of Queensland and Caroline Fewtrell (no relation) for her interest, enthusiasm and assistance in the search for official records of Fewtrell's Early mandarin;

Librarians of the State Library of NSW;

Archivists of NSW Archives;

Librarians of the National Library of Australia, Canberra;

Archivists of the Australian Archives, Canberra;

Archivists of the Noel Butlin Archives Centre at the Australian National University, Canberra;

Librarians of Libraries ACT;

Dr Pat Barkley, Australian citrus expert;

Bill Peterie, for horticultural advice;

Denis Blight, for invaluable agricultural network contacts, relating to the history of citrus crops in India and Pakistan;

Chad Mitcham, researcher extraordinaire, whose skills and contacts led directly to much information relating to Australian citrus growth and exports in the early 20th century and the sourcing of the *Punjab Fruit Journal* from Cornell University;

Tricia Johnson, Sister of Mercy, for alerting me to the writings of Ilia Delio, in exchange for me introducing her to those of Elizabeth Johnson; and

Helen Farrell, Joseph de Riva O'Phelan and Adrian Fordham for thorough, and appropriately challenging, proofreading of advanced drafts of the manuscript.

A particular thanks is due to Australian historians Mark McKenna and David Headon, whose advice on this project I sought at an early stage and who reviewed an advanced version of the manuscript, with wise advice and encouragement. I trust that the final text lives up to their counsel.

A very special thank you is owed to my wife, Christine Lancaster, who has long been aware of my interest in this story and has always encouraged this project. Christine's support and assistance has been evident at many stages along the way, from seemingly endless rambles around places in Shropshire and Kellinghusen, to the very practical of reading and reviewing drafts and accommodating the long preoccupations of the writer. Christine's assistance has at all time been generous and gracious, valuable and valued.

Finally, I would like to thank Stephen Matthews of Ginninderra Press for his confidence in the manuscript and providing the opportunity to share the story of 'George, Elise and a mandarin' with a wider audience.

www.ingramcontent.com/pod-product-compliance
Lightning Source LLC
Chambersburg PA
CBHW070905080526
44589CB00013B/1184